To the chefs, home cooks, friends, family and clients who have supported me; your belief in my dreams, without judgement, has helped to shape this chapter of my life. Because of you, I've been able to write my third book.

This one is for the curious, the passionate, and those who cook to share love and connection. May these recipes bring joy, build confidence, and remind you that the kitchen is where stories are shared and dreams grow.

ONE PAN VIETNAM

Vibrant Vietnamese Recipes for Everyday

THUY DIEM PHAM

photography by Laura Edwards

Quadrille

CONTENTS

6	Introduction
9	Food and Me
10	An Introduction to Cooking Vietnamese
12	The Five Fundamental Flavours
15	The Key to Balance
16	Basic Techniques
20	Basic Equipment
22	Key Ingredients
26	How to Use This Book
28	**Light Bites and Starters**
64	**Soups and Noodles**
90	**Meat**
118	**Fish and Seafood**
134	**Salads and Vegetables**
160	**Sweets**
174	Batch Cooking Condiments
182	Index
189	About the Author
190	Acknowledgements

INTRODUCTION

One Pan Vietnam... every dish using just one pot or pan. Too optimistic? If you'd asked me during my restaurant days, I'd have chuckled and given you a look that said, 'Good luck with that!' My grandmother, with her years of wisdom, would have rolled her eyes at the very thought. Yet today, I couldn't be more thrilled to share that this is not only possible but also a brilliant way to cook.

Vietnamese cuisine is renowned for its complexity: sweet, salty, sour, spicy and bitter flavours all balanced and dancing together. Traditionally, creating these layers involved a kitchen full of ingredients, an array of utensils and more pots than you could count. It was a process that required time, patience and, let's be honest, a willingness to clean up a big mess afterwards. But times have changed, and so must the way we cook. In this book, I am presenting an alternative approach. By using a few clever tweaks and smart shortcuts, you can achieve the same depth of flavour with just one pot. There's no need to sacrifice the flavours we know and love, and the best part is that there's a lot less mess to deal with afterwards.

Growing up, I watched my mum and her friends turn food prep into a lively affair. Every corner of the kitchen would be occupied, every inch of counter space covered with ingredients, and every pot and pan brought into action along with laughter, gossip and even the occasional song! The bigger the mess, the better the dish, or so it seemed. The result was always worth the chaos, but as a kid, the cleaning up afterwards didn't exactly win my heart.

Fast forward to my years running a restaurant kitchen, and I've learned a thing or two about efficiency. In a professional kitchen, every second counts and every action has to be deliberate. I've spent countless hours perfecting workflows, testing recipes and finding ways to save time without compromising flavour. I've done the legwork so you don't have to.

Cooking at home, though, is a completely different experience. It should be about love and care, not about spending hours scrubbing dishes. It's often said that in Asian cultures, food is a form of affection, sometimes in place of words or hugs. Maybe that's why, instead of a hug, you'd find yourself with a bowl of steaming hot, eight-hour noodle soup in front of you. I'm happy to report, though, that our generation is finding a healthier balance between hugs and good noodle soups. A step in the right direction, if you ask me.

Vietnamese cooking has always been labour-intensive, and for good reason. Our country's diverse regions produce ingredients that are unique to their locales. In the past, there was no overnight shipping to bring herbs from the south to the north, so dishes evolved differently based on what was available. Take our national dish, phở. In the south, it's served with an abundance of fresh herbs and has a slightly sweeter broth, while in the north it's more minimalist, with just spring onions (scallions). These differences are a response to the local climate and available produce. In the hot south, cooling down the soup with herbs makes perfect sense, while up north a warmer, more comforting bowl is just what you need on a chilly day. Is one version better than the other? That's for you to decide. But I hope understanding the reasons behind these differences makes you appreciate them more.

One pan cooking is about focusing on what's essential and allowing the ingredients to shine. In my family, nothing was ever wasted in the kitchen. Every ingredient was used with respect, and every step in the cooking process was executed with care. Timings weren't measured by clocks but by sight, sound and smell. Cooking was an art, honed by generations of trial and error. Even with simple ingredients, my mum could create a feast. Five or six different dishes on the table, each one a masterpiece of flavour, made from scratch and always shared with love. Her recipes were never written down; they were passed down through practice and the taste of a perfectly balanced dish. I've done my best to capture that spirit in this book.

This cookbook is a celebration of tradition, but with a modern twist. It's about bringing the incredible flavours of Vietnamese cuisine into your home kitchen with minimal fuss. You'll find recipes inspired by family favourites, restaurant classics and even a few contemporary creations, all adapted to work beautifully with just one pan. Whether you're simmering a rich broth, stir-frying fragrant noodles or caramelizing fish, the goal is to make cooking approachable, enjoyable and, most importantly, delicious.

Cooking with one pot doesn't just simplify the process, it also brings a certain elegance to the act of cooking. There's something so satisfying about creating a dish from start to finish in a single vessel, allowing the flavours to meld and deepen as they cook together. It's a method that feels intentional, almost meditative, as you focus on building layers of flavour with minimal clutter.

But this is about more than just saving time or effort. It's about embracing the joy of cooking in a way that suits modern life, while still respecting the traditions that make Vietnamese food so special. One pan cooking can remind us that less is sometimes more, a philosophy that resonates deeply with Vietnamese culture. It's about simplicity, resourcefulness and making the most of what you have – a mindset passed down through generations.

Whether you're a seasoned cook or just a beginner, I hope this book inspires you to embrace the simplicity and beauty of one pan cooking. With a little creativity and a good recipe, you'll find that one pan is all you need to create dishes that are rich, layered and full of love. After all, less time cleaning means more time enjoying a good meal with those you care about.

FOOD AND ME

My journey with food began in a small village in southern Vietnam, Cầu Ngang, where many of my fondest memories revolve around roaming freely on my grandparents' rice farm, chasing ducks and picking low-hanging fruit from the trees along the way. If the fruit was too high for my little legs, I would climb the tree to reach it. Scars were made, each one worth it! My love for food started early. While that hasn't changed, it has evolved in adulthood. No more climbing trees. Instead, I will travel miles for a good meal and happily spend hours preparing meals for my loved ones.

Growing up, I was surrounded by strong women. They worked with humble ingredients and turned them into amazing dishes; they showed creativity in making do with so little, yet feeding so many. My zero-waste, nose-to-tail approach to cooking is undoubtedly because of this upbringing. They never complained about preparing meals for celebratory events. On the contrary, there was storytelling and laughter. Every movement was instinctive – no hesitation or checking a recipe. They balanced flavours by taste alone. Only ever the occasional mishap, if a particularly juicy bit of gossip had distracted the aunties!

Grandma and her team of aunties could cook for a wedding banquet like it was a quiet lunch service. The only sweat they broke into was from the heat and smoke in the kitchen. It wasn't the biggest space, and there were more chefs than needed, but everyone knew their role. Mine, of course, was tasting.

Life took a dramatic turn when my family relocated to England after the Vietnam War. Adapting to a new culture while holding on to our Vietnamese roots was both challenging and rewarding. My father's courage at sea and our family's resilience have always inspired me to share our story through food. After fulfilling my parents' dream of pursuing higher education, I spent nearly a decade in the advertising industry until I could no longer ignore my true passion. It was calling in more ways than words can explain. I finally plucked up the courage to leave the corporate world and venture into the culinary scene, where the UK's first organic Vietnamese restaurant, the multi-award-winning The Little Viet Kitchen, was born. It was there that I refined my skills and developed a unique approach to Vietnamese cuisine that, thankfully, resonated with our diners.

Now, as a chef consultant to commercial kitchens nationwide, a food writer and, most importantly, a mother to my own little sous chef, my mission has evolved. I still strive to demystify Vietnamese food for home cooks, aiming to make it both accessible and enjoyable, but now I also find so much joy in passing on my knowledge to industry chefs.

All the women in my life, especially my mum, have genuinely shaped who I am today, particularly when it comes to the integrity of food and cooking. Despite years of insisting to myself that I wouldn't be like them, I now see myself truly becoming an auntie in the kitchen. I'm naturally embracing their ways, adding all that I've learned from my time in UK hospitality alongside some of the most talented and amazing chefs in the world.

An Introduction to Cooking Vietnamese

Authenticity is a complicated idea. What does it really mean, and how is it measured? Is there a right or wrong answer? Perhaps. Over the years in the food industry, I've come to terms with this question. As a mother and a Vietnamese chef, I see it as my duty to represent my heritage with integrity and respect. That will always come first. However, the reality is, some adaptations are necessary for the cuisine to grow. It's impractical, expensive and not particularly eco-friendly to always insist on specific ingredients rather than use those grown locally. For some dishes, there really can be no substitute; however, for many there are excellent alternatives that, to my mind, don't impact the 'authenticity' of the dish. Of course, these adjustments have to be made with care, staying true to the core flavours of Vietnamese cooking and, most importantly, with an understanding of why that ingredient was in the dish in the first place.

Accessibility to ingredients often determines whether a dish feels achievable, so throughout this book I've made several tweaks and changes to help you get started. If you're already on this journey, or have a well-stocked local Asian supermarket, I hope you still find them useful, and delicious.

Once people become familiar with the ingredients and techniques, their confidence in the kitchen grows. Suddenly, they're creating dishes that surprise even themselves. And the best part is that sometimes, even when a dish doesn't go exactly to plan, it still tastes incredible. Some of the best recipes are born from happy accidents. Cooking is a journey, and every new dish is a delicious step towards mastering the craft.

Vietnamese food is, to me, the definition of naturally healthy cooking. It's about fresh flavours that honour humble ingredients, brought to life with simple techniques and a bit of patience. Again, take our national dish, phở. It's more than just a bowl of noodle soup. It carries the weight of Vietnamese history and culture in every spoonful. Every time I make it, I'm reminded of how a handful of everyday ingredients, with time, love and care, can come together to make something extraordinary. That's the magic of Vietnamese cooking: flavours simple yet complex that nourish the body and the soul.

Now, let's get started on what makes Vietnamese food so tasty!

THE FIVE FUNDAMENTAL FLAVOURS

Vietnamese food is all about balance. Every recipe is carefully designed to blend the five fundamental flavours; sweet, salty, sour, bitter and spicy. The aim of every dish is to ensure they work together elegantly. They should interact and complement each other, always working to enhance the dish as a whole. Sounds complicated, I know, but it's really not once you break it down.

fermented ingredients like black beans, tofu and shrimp paste, fish sauce remains the heart of it all. It's in our marinades, condiments, soups, stir-fries, salads and even our pickles. In its raw form, fish sauce can be a little intense for those unfamiliar with it, but when used correctly it should never overpower. Instead, it becomes the greatest tool in South East Asian cooking, infusing dishes with that unmistakable Vietnamese flavour.

1. Sweet

Sweetness in Vietnamese cooking isn't just about contrast, it's essential for rounding out and balancing bold, savoury flavours. We achieve this using palm sugar, rock sugar, honey, nước màu caramel sauce, or fruit, such as pineapples. In Western cooking, sweetness is mainly associated with desserts, but in Vietnam it plays a major role in savoury dishes. A spoonful of sugar in a phở broth or nước chấm dipping sauce helps offset the saltiness of fish sauce and brings out the natural sweetness of the ingredients.

2. Salty

I often joke that fish sauce runs through my veins, but the truth is, its pungent saltiness is the backbone of Vietnamese cuisine. It doesn't just enhance the umami, it brings a lovely depth to every dish. While we also build layers of saltiness with soy sauce and

3. Sour

For as long as I can remember, just the thought of sour food like green mango or unripened fruit makes my mouth water. Some might say these are fruit not ready to eat, but in Vietnam we love them for their tartness and crunchy texture. Over time, we've found many delicious ways to enjoy fruit and vegetables at every stage of their ripeness, embracing the sharp, mouth-puckering flavours. Take mango, for example. When green, it's the most incredible salad ingredient, and when ripe it makes for a wonderful dessert or the perfect addition to a fruit platter, and takes your smoothies and cocktails to another level.

Sourness isn't just something we enjoy on its own, it plays a crucial role in balancing your meal. It keeps Vietnamese food light and refreshing, cuts through richness, balances fatty cuts of meat and wakes up the palate with every bite. That zesty, bright note is what lifts a dish and makes it truly come alive. So, next time you see a wedge of lime served with a Vietnamese dish, don't ignore it... Squeeze it in. Trust the process!

4. Bitter

Bitterness can sound much scarier than it actually is. I often wonder if it's a flavour profile we learn to appreciate over time, as it's not something children tend to enjoy. Bitter melon comes to mind: the classic 'love it or hate it' ingredient. This vegetable is so packed with nutrients that our parents would start feeding it to us from a young age, hoping we'd grow up to love it. Despite plenty of resistance and doubt, most of us eventually embrace its bitterness, even crave it, and keep it in our diets. In fact, it's often one of those nostalgic dishes that bring back memories of childhood home-cooked meals. That's what I love about food. It's not just about the taste, but the journey, the love, and the memories attached to it, even when it's something as unapologetically bitter as bitter melon.

Like the other four flavours, bitterness has its own role in balancing Vietnamese cuisine. It's often found in fresh herbs, which is why, when a recipe calls for them, you shouldn't skip them. If you see fresh leaves in your Vietnamese dish, know that they're not just garnish, they're the secret ingredient that ties everything together and makes a meal complete.

5. Spicy

Spicy is definitely my favourite of them all. No meal is ever truly complete until that spice kick hits. It's the flavour that separates the tough from the weak. I'm even partial to a little chilli in my dessert!

In all seriousness, spice in Vietnamese cooking isn't just about heat, it's about the aromatics, the warmth and depth it adds to the dish. It shouldn't overpower, but instead provide a subtle, smooth tingle. It's never heat for the sake of heat; it's finding that perfect balance that makes each bite exciting and flavourful.

THE KEY TO BALANCE

Balance in cooking has always felt instinctive to me, something I never had to overthink. Naturally following my mum and grandma around the kitchen from a very young age, I learned by watching them closely and by completing the tasks they set for me. Without realizing it, I was absorbing invaluable skills and techniques.

I remember Mum telling me that achieving balance isn't about strict measurements, it's about tasting, adjusting and trusting your senses. This intuitive approach to flavour is what makes Vietnamese food so adaptable, allowing each cook to tailor a recipe to their own taste while maintaining the integrity of the dish.

A meal might have a sweetness to it, but it's always countered by saltiness and acidity. A rich, hearty broth is always paired with fresh herbs and a squeeze of lime. Spicy dishes don't just bring heat, they carry depth, layering different flavours and aromas. Once you understand how the five fundamental tastes work together, Vietnamese cooking becomes less of a mystery and more of an instinct. And the best part? You can adjust each element to suit your own palate, just as we do in Vietnam; cooking isn't about rigid rules.

BASIC TECHNIQUES

What makes a cuisine unique isn't just the ingredients or spices, there's often significant overlap across cultures. The true mark of a cuisine lies in its preparation – the techniques used to create distinctive textures and flavours. Many of these methods are surprisingly simple, yet we often assume they must be difficult because the results taste so incredible!

Traditionally in rural Vietnam, we'd cook over an open fire built from mud, with a simple rack to hold our pots. We didn't have many, just a few in different shapes and sizes, so dishes were created around the tools we had or, sometimes, the tools were shaped by the dishes we needed to make.

These days, it can feel overwhelming to shop for a long list of ingredients and a whole new set of equipment just to try one recipe. I understand that stepping into a new cuisine isn't just about wanting to eat it, it's about confidence in the process. So, here are some of the key techniques used in Vietnamese cooking to familiarize yourself with.

Stir-frying

Maybe I'm not alone in this, but stir-frying is my go-to for everyday cooking, and for good reason. It's quick and easy, and effortlessly scales from a single portion to a meal for ten. But the main reason I love it? Stir-frying is simply the best way to cook fresh greens. A quick flash in the pan locks in their vibrant colour, keeps their crisp texture and preserves all their goodness. If you've ever had rau muống xào tỏi – garlic morning glory stir-fry – you'll know exactly what I mean. If you haven't, it's a must-try! Otherwise, give the cavolo nero recipe on page 151 a go.

The key is to avoid overcooking or undercooking while ensuring everything goes from pan to plate in minutes. Follow these simple tips, and in no time you'll be cooking like an Asian auntie!:

– *A very hot pan and a high smoke point oil, like vegetable oil, are essential. For meat and seafood, the intense heat creates a beautiful char without making them tough. Harder vegetables, like carrots, go in first, while delicate greens, like kale and pak choi, should be added last.*
– *Cook proteins and vegetables separately, season them individually, then bring everything together at the end with just a few final seconds on the heat, no more.*
– *Never overcrowd the pan, or you'll end up steaming instead of stir-frying.*
– *Have all your ingredients prepped before you start cooking.*

Braising

Braising is one of those techniques that makes you feel like a magician in the kitchen. It takes the toughest cuts, like beef shin, brisket, pork neck or shoulder, and turns them into something unbelievably tender, rich and full of deep flavour. It's also incredibly forgiving. Once everything is in the pot and the impurities are skimmed off, the hard work is done. The heat takes care of the rest.

The perfect example is thịt kho trứng, a traditional dish of braised pork and eggs in coconut water. To me, this dish tastes of home. It's not lobster, and certainly not caviar, but ask any Viet to choose, and I'm sure this would win hands down. Some dishes have that nostalgic power that money can't buy. Here, the sweet coconut water combined with fish sauce infuse right to the centre of the meat, creating a subtle yet deep flavour all at once. My goodness, this is comfort food at its best! Try it on page 100; you'll thank me later.

So, what's the secret? Low and slow.
- The magic starts with searing the meat to build a deep, caramelized crust, an essential layer of flavour.
- Then come the aromatics: garlic, shallots, lemongrass and spices, releasing their fragrance before the liquid is added.
- Once covered, a gentle simmer does the work, breaking down tough fibres and creating a silky, rich sauce.
- Patience is everything. Rush it, and you won't get the same results. But trust me, it's always worth it!

Steaming

Steaming is my go-to healthy option when I don't fancy a salad or have time for an eight-hour bone broth noodle soup. A technique so simple it almost seems too easy. Can it really create something that flavourful? If you've ever had bánh cuốn, those delicate rice rolls filled with pork, mushrooms and glass noodles, you'll know it can. Of course, it's then served with fresh herbs and nước chấm. Everything I want on a plate.

This technique requires no oil and no frying, just pure, gentle heat that locks in moisture, keeping everything light, fresh and full of natural flavour. The key to steaming is controlled heat and good airflow. Here are some guidelines to keep in mind:

- Always bring the water to a rolling boil before adding your ingredients.
- A bamboo steamer is best as it absorbs excess moisture, keeping food from getting soggy. A metal or ceramic set-up works well too, or see page 21 for how to create one using bowls and a standard pan.
- Leave space between the food pieces so the steam can circulate evenly.
- Watch it closely and you'll have delicate, juicy results every time.

Grilling (broiling) and Roasting

Grilling fills the streets of Vietnam with an aroma that leads you to your next meal. Maybe it's just me, but I'm always hungry when I'm there. Street vendors turn simple, everyday ingredients into something unforgettable. Often, the best meal isn't from a fancy restaurant, but from an auntie or uncle who has spent decades perfecting one dish. It makes you think about all the choices we have in the West and how they've shaped what we expect from a meal. I love the focus and dedication to mastering a single dish. And when vendors get it right, they really get it right. There's no need to second-guess your next meal in Vietnam. It's almost always guaranteed to be good!

Fire cooking has always been at the heart of Vietnamese street food, often on the most modest set-ups. The smoke rising in the distance, the irresistible aroma pulling you in, and the deep, smoky flavours that keep you coming back. The skill is undeniable. Vendors churn out hundreds of perfectly charred skewers, keeping them at just the right temperature until they sell out. It all comes down to three things: careful prep, good heat control and well-marinated meat.

There's no real secret to great grilling, just a few things to keep in mind. Once you understand the process and repeat it a few times, it becomes second nature:

– The key is mastering heat control and ingredient placement, whether on a barbecue (grill) or in an oven. Food should be placed close to the heat for a quick sear of meat or a blistering of vegetables. If using an oven, consistent heat circulation is crucial, so always preheat the oven before putting in your dish.
– Marinating meat beforehand is key in Vietnamese cooking if you have the time. Once you've tried it, you'll want to make time. The difference in flavour and texture is undeniable from the first bite. Don't waste leftover marinade. Use it to baste the meat as it cooks for even more flavour.
– Always finish with a blast of high heat for crispy roast chicken or perfect pork belly crackling.
– And whatever you do, let the meat rest before slicing. This lets the juices settle, making every bite better.

Simmering

This technique requires patience, consistency and dedication. A true testament to this method is Vietnam's national dish, phở, where the broth is gently simmered for hours with beef bones, charred onions, ginger and spices. The result? A deeply umami, aromatic broth that's clear, fragrant, and the perfect base for rice noodles, fresh herbs and thinly sliced beef. If you know phở, you'll know that the clarity of the broth is everything. Achieving that clarity is only possible with a low and slow simmer. High heat will break down delicate ingredients and turn the broth cloudy, so control is key.

For a perfect simmer:
– Start on a high heat to bring the pot to the boil, then reduce to low or medium-low, letting it quietly cook away while you get on with other tasks. This allows the flavours to develop slowly, so don't rush it.
– Give the ingredients time to work their magic and you'll be rewarded with a beautifully balanced, flavour-packed dish that's worth every minute of the wait.

BASIC EQUIPMENT

While it's true that a bad workman always blames their tools, when it comes to cooking, having the right tools truly makes a difference. I'm not advocating for a kitchen packed with every gadget imaginable or enough pots and pans to outfit a restaurant. Instead, I firmly believe in investing in a handful of high-quality pieces that elevate both the preparation and presentation of your dishes.

The right pot or pan can be transformative. It helps you achieve the ideal texture, maintains precise temperatures and, most importantly, gives you control over the final outcome of your dish. With these essentials, you'll not only execute traditional Vietnamese recipes to perfection but also unlock a versatility that will help in your everyday cooking.

Now, I have to admit, I do love cookware. Give me the same pot in every available colour, and I'm very happy! But I've had to learn to strike a balance between indulgence and practicality. While I might daydream about a rainbow array of clay pots, the truth is that being thoughtful about your selection of tools can take you far without overwhelming your cupboards.

So, in this chapter, I'm sharing the essentials. These are the tools I rely on in my kitchen, not just for Vietnamese cuisine but for everyday cooking in general. They're versatile, durable and timeless; a perfect mix of function and flair. Let's dive into what you really need to create authentic, flavourful dishes without drowning in a sea of cookware.

Essential or Useful Tools

BAKING TRAYS: A medium one for roasting vegetables, plus a deep one for whole birds and meat joints.

BASTING BRUSH: For that golden, crispy finish on roasts, barbecues and pastries.

CAST IRON GRIDDLE: Perfect for indoor grilling. It holds high heat for beautiful sear marks and smoky flavour in pork chops, steak or vegetables. Preheat thoroughly and avoid moving food too soon as patience gives the best char. Be warned: it gets deliciously smoky, but it's worth it.

CLAY POT: The secret to rich caramelization and deep umami in dishes like cá kho tộ and thịt kho. Clay pots distribute heat slowly and evenly, keeping meat and fish tender while trapping moisture. Soak for 30 minutes before use to prevent cracking, then heat gently and let flavours build slowly, just like grandma's cooking.

FINE MESH PASTA/NOODLE STRAINER BASKET: Perfect for portioning noodles and draining excess moisture, so your broth stays rich and undiluted.

FINE MESH SIEVE (STRAINER): Helps to keep your broths clear and your flour smooth.

HAND MIXER: A reliable helper for whisking, blending and making smooth batters without the arm workout.

MANDOLIN: Essential for shredding vegetables and the occasional fruit into delicate, even textures. Your secret weapon when making perfect Vietnamese salads and pickles.

PESTLE AND MORTAR: Unlocks the best flavours in spices, garlic and pastes. Sometimes, old-school is still best!

RICE COOKER: The easiest way to get perfectly fluffy rice every time. Essential for any kitchen, but especially so for Vietnamese cuisine.

SHARP KNIVES: A must. A good blade ensures clean cuts, better textures and an easier time in the kitchen. I rely on three: a paring knife for precision, a chef's knife for all-purpose chopping, and a bread knife – not just for bread, but for slicing chewy spring rolls, summer rolls and carving roasted meats, among many other jobs.

FINE MESH SKIMMER: A priceless tool that skims away impurities with ease, making it essential for achieving a clear broth. It's also handy for deep-frying, as the fine mesh allows excess oil to drain away as you lift.

SMALL FOOD PROCESSOR: A cheap, easy-to-clean food processor is a lifesaver for batch prep; from spice pastes to marinades.

SMALL OFFSET PALETTE KNIFE: A quiet kitchen hero. From flipping delicate items to checking when your elements are ready, it helps you cook with finesse.

STEAMER (BAMBOO OR METAL): Great for gently cooking vegetables, fish and dumplings. To create a steamer if you don't have one, take your largest saucepan with a lid, or a small stockpot, and place a bowl upside down on the bottom. Fill with water to just below the top of the bowl then place a second bowl, the correct way up, securely on top of the first. Then put the lid on and continue as for a steamer.

HEAVY-BASED LIDDED CASSEROLE (DUTCH OVEN): For slow-cooked dishes that develop rich, deep flavours with minimal effort.

STOCKPOT: Non-negotiable for Asian cooking. Essential for bone broths and batch cooking. If you can, get one with a steaming rack – it's very convenient for dumplings, buns and seafood.

TONGS: Your extra pair of hands when flipping, turning, tossing, gripping, lifting, plating and handling hot ingredients with precision.

WOODEN CHOPPING (CUTTING) BOARD: Sturdy, safe and kinder to your knives and hands. Chopping should be a joy, not a struggle. If you make sure to wash them thoroughly after each use, then they're safer than plastic ones too.

Basic Equipment

KEY INGREDIENTS

Quick and easy cooking isn't about taking shortcuts or cutting corners, it's about being prepared. A well-stocked larder is the secret to making bold, flavourful Vietnamese dishes with minimal effort. For me, that means having my essential pantry ingredients on hand and, most importantly, making my homemade sauces in big batches. Yes, they take time upfront, but trust me, that effort pays off tenfold when you can whip up a delicious meal in minutes. Cooking smart means you get all the flavour without spending hours in the kitchen, because good food should never be compromised by a lack of time. So, before we dive into *One Pan Vietnam*, let's start with the foundations and batch-make some essentials. This will change the way you cook Vietnamese food forever.

Storecupboard Essentials

A well-stocked pantry is the backbone of Vietnamese cooking, providing the essential building blocks for the cuisine's signature balance of sweet, sour, salty, bitter and spicy flavours. Staples like fish sauce, soy sauce and rice vinegar are not just condiments, they're foundational elements that infuse dishes with depth and authenticity. Whether it's the light sweetness of golden cane sugar or the creamy richness of coconut milk, each ingredient plays a pivotal role in creating the harmony of flavours that is the essence of Vietnamese cuisine. While fresh herbs add brightness, these pantry essentials ensure every dish resonates with the comforting and complex flavours that define Vietnamese home cooking.

COCONUT MILK: A creamy, dairy-free alternative that adds richness to many dishes, but principally to desserts and curries.

COCONUT WATER: A secret meat tenderizer with natural sugars, adding a gentle sweetness to savoury dishes. Perfect for stews and braising; or, if you're in Vietnam, drink it fresh, straight from the tree!

CORNFLOUR (CORNSTARCH): This handy thickening agent is perfect for adding body to noodle soups, and making your crispy chicken wings even crispier!

CRISPY FRIED SHALLOTS: A finishing touch that adds a delicious crunch to a dish.

FISH SAUCE: The cornerstone of Vietnamese cuisine, fish sauce adds depth and umami. Nước mắm is raw fish sauce, made from fermented anchovies, while nước chấm (see page 175) is a dipping sauce made by mixing nước mắm with lime juice, sugar, garlic, chilli and water for balance.

GOLDEN CANE SUGAR: Preferred over white sugar for its mellow sweetness and subtle caramel notes, golden cane sugar blends more naturally into Vietnamese cooking. It enhances savoury, sour and spicy flavours without overpowering them, giving sauces and broths a deeper, more rounded finish.

HONEY: A versatile sweetener, honey is often used as a substitute for sugar when a more delicate floral or fruity note is desired. It works wonders in barbecue (grill) marinades.

LIME JUICE: From a bottle for ease or freshly squeezed, lime juice provides a natural sour note for sauces, and can be used for curing and pickling.

OYSTER SAUCE: Rich and meaty, it brings a lovely thickness and depth to sauces. While similar to soy sauce, it has a distinct umami flavour that enhances stir-fries and marinades and brings that deep, sticky char to your meats.

PAPRIKA: Not traditional but adds colour, gentle sweetness and smokiness to curries and marinades. It complements turmeric and lemongrass, and boosts savoury depth alongside fish sauce, garlic and shallots.

RICE AND RICE NOODLES: A staple in almost every Vietnamese meal – whether it's jasmine or glutinous rice, rice vermicelli or flat rice (phở) noodles – they are the unsung heroes that soak up all those delicious sauces and flavours, adding a little extra balance and nutrition too.

RICE WINE VINEGAR: A key ingredient in pickling.

ROCK SUGAR: Rock sugar has a mild, clean sweetness. It dissolves slowly, making it ideal for simmering broths and braises, creating a smooth, glossy finish. It's the secret ingredient in many Vietnamese soups and stews.

SESAME OIL: The Asian olive oil! Its rich and nutty flavour makes almost any dish that little bit better. My meat marinades are never without it, and any vegetable roast is improved by it.

SHRIMP PASTE OR UMAMI PASTE: Add a savoury depth to soups, sauces and marinades.

SOY SAUCE: Light soy is saltier and thinner, used for seasoning rather than adding colour. Dark soy is thicker, less salty and slightly sweet, perfect for adding richness and colour to braises, stir-fries and marinades.

TAMARIND CONCENTRATE: A key ingredient in many Vietnamese dishes. Just a small amount packs a bold, tangy punch, balancing sweet and sour notes beautifully. Perfect for lifting salads, sauces and stir-fries with its natural kick.

Fresh Ingredients

Fresh ingredients are the soul of Vietnamese cooking, and herbs in particular carry the identity of each dish. Whether it's a few torn leaves of Thai basil or a scattering of chopped coriander (cilantro), these final touches complete the flavour journey. Always choose fresh where possible to capture the clean, layered balance we're known for. Even in small amounts, these ingredients matter. Where traditional herbs like Vietnamese mint aren't accessible, don't be afraid to substitute with the closest flavour profile, mint. Or coriander with parsley, for instance, makes a good stand-in.

CHILLIES: Fresh or dried, they find their way on, in or accompanying almost every dish. Want to keep it authentic? Bird's eye chillies should be your baseline heat level.

CHIVES: Delicate yet punchy, chives add a mild garlic-onion flavour to soups, sauces, dumplings and savoury pancakes, and can be used as a garnish or folded into fillings. They are a staple in gardens as they're quick to grow and thrive in small spaces.

GARLIC: Essential for creating a foundation of flavour in countless recipes. Whether raw, fried or roasted, it brings depth and added flavour to every dish. Not sure if we love it more than the French do, but it's a core ingredient in every Vietnamese kitchen.

GINGER: Ginger adds a warm, zesty kick to savoury dishes, especially common in chicken and fish recipes. It also aids digestion, making it a delicious staple in desserts and drinks too.

HERBS: The likes of coriander (cilantro), Thai basil, mint, dill, chives and spring onions (scallions) bring a freshness and flavour to the plate. The non-traditional in this list are accessible alternatives that I feel best fit the profiles of traditional Vietnamese herbs, which can sometimes be hard to find.

LEMONGRASS: Unbeatable aromatic flavour, perfect for marinades, soups and stir-fries. It's a signature ingredient in Vietnamese cuisine. Rarely the star, but often the ingredient that ties everything together.

LIME LEAVES: An essential ingredient for curries and stews, fresh lime leaves add a fragrant citrus note to any dish. When thinly sliced, they bring a fresh, aromatic element to salads as well.

ROASTED PEANUTS: A must-have for Vietnamese salads and desserts, adding extra crunch and depth. If you ever get the chance to try them freshly blanched, please do. Once you taste their natural flavour, you'll see them as legumes and never look at them the same way again. Especially when you've seen them grown underground like potatoes!

SHALLOTS: Sweeter than onions, shallots in Vietnam are always the red variety, but throughout the recipes I call for either regular shallots or the elongated echalion, or banana shallot, which is larger and easier to peel.

SPRING ONIONS (SCALLIONS): A key garnish, used raw, stir-fried, braised or pickled. In Vietnam they are not only affordable and versatile, they are symbolic of luck, growth and renewal because of their resilience – the ability to sprout even in the shade.

HOW TO USE THIS BOOK

Does this book do exactly what it says on the tin? Absolutely! But before you dive into the mouth-watering recipes, let's chat about what makes my one-pan approach different from the usual. I want to manage your expectations and avoid any surprises along the way. The goal here was always to create dishes that are both delicious and approachable, whether they're quick to put together or require a bit more finesse. The mission? Only one pan, and yes, I've managed to hit the brief. Only, it wasn't as difficult as you might expect.

Vietnamese cuisine often doesn't require more than a single pan. When we have the luxury of using more pans for convenience, we tend to overdo it. This book is all about proving that you can get exceptional results with less. Ok, so there might be an occasional mixing bowl or two, but trust me, you'll end up with meals that look like you've used every pan in the kitchen! You'll only need one main pan to cook these dishes. With a few rinses in between, of course, as I can't make it too easy for you. My mum would always have a muslin cloth hanging from her left hip, there to quickly wipe pans clean and quickly dry them between wipes.

Now, I know one pan cooking often means 'throw everything in and call it a day', but here's the thing: however it's prepped, I love to plate my dishes. For me, the presentation is almost as important as the flavours, showing respect for both the recipe and the effort you've put in. So, get ready to cook with intention, creativity and a touch of love, because that is what makes the difference in a dish, regardless of the recipe.

This book isn't just a collection of recipes, it's an invitation to explore bold Vietnamese flavours with ease. No complicated techniques, no endless washing up, just one pan, great ingredients and a whole lot of love (and fish sauce).

Some recipes are very quick, while others are for those days when you have a little more time to spend making something extra special. Start with the simple ones, then indulge at the weekend with something slow-cooked and flavour-packed. Let food be your love language and truly turn your kitchen into the heart of your home.

Batch Cook It

Before you cook a single recipe, I strongly recommend that you batch cook the five key sauces from the chapter starting on page 174. Sauces are the foundation of Vietnamese cooking and are the difference between good and amazing. My restaurant days taught me that the smoother your prep, the smoother your cook. Bringing that mindset into your home kitchen means getting ahead where you can. Stock up, batch cook and get your flavour bases ready. Then, as you go through the recipes, I'll show you how to build on them, tweak them and create something new and exciting every time.

Make it Veggie

Many recipes in this book can be made vegetarian and often vegan without losing their essence, and for most it would be hard to argue that they don't taste just as good, or even better! A veggie twist can bring a whole new dimension to a dish, with fresh, light flavours that shine through in a different way. For recipes with the option *Make it Veggie*, I offer fish, tofu and/or vegetable substitutes for the meat. For others it's simply a matter of swapping the fish sauce for light soy sauce (vegan fish sauce is also available, though I prefer light soy), or using vegan oyster sauce or mushroom sauce, for the recipe to be vegetarian or vegan. The beauty of Vietnamese cuisine lies in its layers of flavours and textures, and ingredients are often more easily adaptable than you might think.

Serving Suggestions

For certain recipes, I'll suggest traditional Vietnamese serving styles or pairings that I think will complement the dish. I hope these tips will be useful for your meal planning.

I see recipes as guides, not rules. If you need to tweak something to suit your taste, go for it. It's your kitchen, your rules – although I take no responsibility for the outcome! Many of us grew up eating versions of dishes shaped by family tastebuds. They may not be 100 per cent traditional, but they are still authentic, especially to you. They have simply been adapted to your tastes by those who know you best. That's why they'll always be your favourite, no matter where life takes you. Hopefully, these dishes will become part of your own family traditions, evolving over time.

As you cook your way through *One Pan Vietnam*, I hope you find joy in the clean simplicity and depth of Vietnamese flavours. More than that, I hope this book inspires you to bring a piece of Vietnam into your home and share this beautiful cuisine with your loved ones.

LIGHT BITES AND STARTERS

BÁNH MÌ NƯỚNG TRÁI BƠ

AVOCADO TOAST

TAKES 25 MINUTES — SERVES 2

Avocado toast is a weekend favourite in my family, but this Vietnamese-inspired version is so good, we often make it during the week too. Rich avocado pairs with the sweet and savoury taste of lạp xưởng sausage, fresh blistered cherry tomatoes, and soft, creamy scrambled eggs, creating a perfect balance of flavours and textures. Simple yet satisfying, this dish feels like a special treat any day of the week.

2 large eggs
2 pinches of salt
2 ripe avocados
3 tbsp olive oil
2 shallots, finely diced
5g (⅙oz) coriander (cilantro), stalks and leaves finely chopped
Juice of ½ lime
3 Vietnamese lạp xưởng sausages, diced (or 100g/3½oz chorizo)
16 cherry tomatoes
2 garlic cloves, finely chopped
1 tsp fish sauce
1 tsp honey
2 pinches of coarsely ground black pepper
5g (⅙oz) dill, finely chopped
2 large slices of sourdough bread
10g (¼oz) butter
2 tsp light soy sauce

In a bowl, whisk the eggs with the salt and set aside.

In another bowl, mash the avocado flesh with 1 tablespoon of olive oil, the shallots, coriander and lime juice. Leave the mixture chunky for texture. Set aside.

Heat a small frying pan (skillet) without oil and char the diced lạp xưởng sausages for 30 seconds until they turn a bright, translucent red (or, if using chorizo, until it releases its dark red oil and turns crisp). Remove from the pan and set aside. To the same pan, add the remaining 2 tablespoons of olive oil and cook the cherry tomatoes for 2 minutes without stirring. Then add the garlic, fish sauce, honey and black pepper, cooking for an additional 3 minutes until the tomatoes are blistered. Stir in the dill. Transfer to a bowl and set aside.

Toast the sourdough slices and place on your plates.

Wipe the pan clean and melt the butter over a medium heat. Add the whisked eggs and lower the heat. Stir gently in circular motions with a spatula for 50–60 seconds, until creamy, soft lumps form.

Spread the avocado mixture on the sourdough, add the scrambled eggs, then top with the blistered tomatoes and charred sausage. Finally, drizzle over the soy sauce.

Serving Suggestion
For a spicy kick, drizzle with chilli oil or add a few dashes of chilli sauce.

Make it Veggie
Switch out the sausage for smoked tofu, and the fish sauce for light soy sauce.

GỎI CUỐN TÔM & NẤM RỪNG

PRAWN AND WILD MUSHROOM AUTUMN ROLLS

TAKES 30 MINUTES — MAKES 8

I eat summer rolls – gỏi cuốn – all year round. I'll happily wrap up whatever I have on hand, and I'll take on any challenge when it comes to rolling rice paper. If you can eat it, I can roll it. But I've often wondered, what would I need to tweak to turn them into autumn rolls? Perhaps if I steamed the summer rolls and warmed the dish up? You can probably see where this is heading… this recipe was born one lazy Sunday, and I love it!

Autumn is peak mushroom season, with so many varieties offering up delicate textures and earthy depths to a dish. They're quick to cook, absorb all the surrounding flavours – hello, nước chấm – and pair beautifully with prawns. These rolls are almost too pretty to eat. Almost.

If you're still mastering your rolling skills, don't worry, they'll still taste perfect even if they don't quite look it.

8 sheets of rice paper, 22cm (8½ inches) diameter
20 (about 140g/5oz) cooked king prawns (jumbo shrimp), halved
200g (7oz) wild mushrooms, julienned
50g (1¾oz) chives, left whole

TO GARNISH AND SERVE
200ml (7fl oz) nước chấm (see page 175)
200ml (7fl oz) chilli and lemongrass oil (see page 179)
4 tbsp crispy fried shallots (see page 180 for homemade)

Place a sheet of rice paper on a flat surface, then use a clean J-cloth (food cloth) dipped in cold water to gently dampen both sides.

Add the filling about one-third from the bottom: layer 5 halved prawns, a small handful of mushroom and a few chives.

Fold the bottom edge over the filling, then fold in the sides and roll tightly to seal. Repeat to make 8 rolls.

Set up a steamer and steam the rolls for 5 minutes, until the rice paper is soft and the filling is warmed through.

Slice each roll into bite-sized pieces. Drizzle with nước chấm and chilli and lemongrass oil, and finish with a generous sprinkle of crispy fried shallots.

Make it Veggie
Double the mushroom quantity and leave out the prawns.

BÁNH DẸT PHỞ BÒ

'BEEF PHỞ' FLATBREAD WRAP

TAKES 30 MINUTES, PLUS MARINATING — SERVES 2

This dish combines tender rib-eye steak marinated in aromatic five-spice, with soft Greek flatbread, bringing together a delicious fusion of flavours and textures. Though not a traditional Vietnamese recipe, it draws inspiration from the rich, fragrant elements of phở, Vietnam's national dish. The steak's seasoning, paired with fresh herbs and a tangy dipping sauce, captures the essence of Vietnamese cuisine, offering a mouth-watering meal, with a modern twist.

1 tsp five-spice powder
1 tbsp light soy sauce
1 tbsp fish sauce
2 tbsp sesame oil
2 rib-eye beef steaks, about 250g (9oz) each
1 tbsp vegetable oil
2 Greek flatbreads
20g (¾oz) beansprouts
10g (⅓oz) Thai basil, leaves chopped
10g (⅓oz) coriander (cilantro), stalks and leaves chopped
10g (⅓oz) mint leaves, chopped
1 red onion, thinly sliced
1 red chilli, thinly sliced
4 tsp hoisin sauce
4 tsp sriracha sauce
½ lime, halved

To a large bowl, add the five-spice, soy sauce, fish sauce and sesame oil. Add the steaks and rub the marinade in evenly. Leave to marinate for at least 20 minutes, or up to 3 hours in the fridge if you have the time (removing from the fridge 30 minutes before cooking to bring to room temperature).

Heat the vegetable oil in a large pan over a medium-high heat. Sear the steaks for 1–2 minutes on each side for medium, or longer if preferred. Remove from the pan and leave to rest for a few minutes before slicing into strips.

Wipe the pan clean and warm each flatbread for about 1 minute. On each flatbread, layer the beansprouts, chopped herbs, steak strips, red onion and chilli. Lastly, drizzle the hoisin sauce and sriracha across the top, and squeeze over the lime juice to taste.

Fold the sides of each flatbread over the filling, then roll tightly into a wrap, securing with a toothpick if needed.

Make it Veggie
Substitute the beef with 500g (1lb 2oz) firm smoked tofu, cut into 3cm (1¼ inch) slices. Skip the marinating step and fry over a medium heat for 5 minutes each side.

GỎI CUỐN THỊT NGUỘI

CHARCUTERIE SUMMER ROLLS

TAKES 30 MINUTES — MAKES 12

What can you roll in rice paper? Well, pretty much anything – the list is endless. Fresh and colourful, these summer rolls are the perfect one-bite canapé to impress your guests. Inspired by the classic Vietnamese combo of prawns and pork, this recipe provides a new twist... cured meats. And let me tell you, they're absolutely delicious. These elegant little canapés will be perfect at your next gathering, or even as a fun addition to a cheeseboard.

12 sheets of summer roll rice paper
200g (7oz) mixed Italian salad leaves
200g (7oz) cured charcuterie
1 cucumber, julienned
1 carrot, julienned
1 red (bell) pepper, deseeded and julienned
25g (1oz) coriander (cilantro), leaves picked
25g (1oz) mint, leaves picked
200ml (7fl oz) nước chấm (see page 175), to serve

Place a sheet of rice paper on a flat surface, then use a clean J-cloth (food cloth) dipped in cold water to gently dampen both sides.

Arrange a selection of the mixed leaves, cured charcuterie, cucumber, carrot, red pepper, coriander and mint leaves neatly along the centre of the first sheet of rice paper.

Fold the rice paper in like an envelope, bringing the sides towards the centre with roughly 3cm (1¼ inch) folds. Fold the top edge down, then roll tightly from the bottom to the top to secure the filling.

Repeat the process with the remaining rice paper sheets and filling. Your rolls will get better as you do more, I promise. So don't give up!

Serve with a generous helping of nước chấm.

Make it Veggie
Substitute the charcuterie for 300g (10½oz) firm tofu. Cut it into thin (2cm/¾ inch) slices and pan-fry over a medium heat for 5 minutes each side. Once cooled, cut into julienne.

MASTERING RICE PAPER

Made from just rice, tapioca, salt and water, rice paper is one of the most versatile ingredients in Vietnamese cooking. But handling it? That's another story. It's delicate. It's unpredictable. And it rarely does what you want... Until one day, it just does. The good news? Even when your rolls aren't perfect, they'll still taste great. Trust me, I've been there.

When I tell my mum I'm teaching a class about rolling gỏi cuốn, she side-eyes me. A wordless response. To her, it's second nature. She's long forgotten the learning curve. She had no recipes or cooking classes – just time, repetition and patience. Family meals involved helping Grandma set the table, then watching as the adults reached in, wet their rice paper, rolled with precision. It looked like choreography, all smiles, laughter, and food shared in rhythm. The basics of happiness really.

As you struggle, you know what you need: longer arms, faster hands and the skills to take control of the rice paper. But there's no shortcut. No cheat code. Only practice. One roll after another. Hundreds later and then suddenly, one day, without even thinking, you realize you're the master of the rice paper at last. Here are tips to get you started.

Learn to read your rice paper
Know when it's soft, when it's too firm, and when it's just right; flexible, elastic and ready. People think rice paper is fragile because it's thin, but that's not quite true. Hydrated properly, it's stronger than it looks, but you must still learn how far you can push it.

Don't soak it in water
I know the internet says otherwise, but never fully submerge it, especially if you're just starting out. Warm water softens it too quickly, and you lose control before you've even started, so use cold water instead. Wet the paper lightly, and wait 8–10 seconds. The rice paper should be soft but not soggy at all, and your plate should stay dry the whole way through.

Don't panic
Take your time. Fold in your fillings neatly, and roll it tight like you mean it.

Keep it snug and airtight
When rolling, push out any air bubbles. They're the enemy, and you don't want fillings slipping out mid-bite. Your goal is a roll that holds its shape – even when dunked in sauce.

Wherever you're at on the journey, don't give up
If it takes 20 tries, let it take 20. If it takes 220? Then so be it. That magic moment will come. And when it does, you'll feel like a true Vietnamese auntie. It's a small skill, but once you've cracked it, it stays with you forever, and you'll pass it on with pride. More importantly, you'll have earned your auntie badge.

CHẢ GIÒ GÀ CHIÊN

FRIED CHICKEN SPRING ROLLS

TAKES 45 MINUTES — MAKES 16

This version of the classic Vietnamese spring roll originates from the south of the country. These spring rolls are enjoyed year-round but hold special significance during festivities and family gatherings. Traditionally made with minced pork and prawns, their versatility allows for chicken as a delicious, lighter alternative. Known for their crispy texture and flavourful filling, they are often paired with a tangy fish dipping sauce or, like me, pair it with the crab, kohlrabi and dill mustard salad on page 139.

16 rice paper sheets
1 egg, lightly beaten
500ml (17fl oz/2 generous cups) vegetable oil
Nước chấm (see page 175), to serve

FOR THE FILLING
500g (1lb 2oz) minced (ground) chicken (20% fat)
200g (7oz) brown and white crab meat
100g (3½oz) drained, canned water chestnuts, chopped
6 spring onions (scallions), finely chopped
100g (3½oz) glass noodles, cooked according to the packet instructions, then chopped
50g (1¾oz) dried shiitake mushrooms, soaked, drained and chopped
4 eggs
2 tbsp sugar
2 tsp fish sauce
2 tbsp sesame oil
1 chicken stock (bouillon) cube, crumbled
1 tbsp salt
2 tbsp coarsely ground black pepper

Ensure your filling ingredients, especially the noodles and mushrooms, are as dry as possible, to prevent the rice paper tearing or bubbling, then add all the filling ingredients to a food processor and pulse for 20–25 seconds. It should be well mixed but still with a slightly chunky texture.

Place a sheet of rice paper on a flat surface, then use a clean J-cloth (food cloth) dipped in cold water to gently dampen both sides.

Spoon 50–60g (1¾–2oz) of filling in a horizontal line across the centre of the rice paper. Fold the sides inward, then bring up the bottom edge to cover the filling. Roll tightly into a neat cylinder, sealing the edge with a little of the egg. Repeat with remaining rice papers and filling.

Heat the vegetable oil in a deep frying pan (skillet) over a medium heat until it reaches 175°C (347°F). To check if the oil is ready, dip a wooden chopstick into it; if bubbles form around the chopstick, it's ready.

Fry the spring rolls in batches, turning occasionally, until crisp and golden all over, about 5–7 minutes. Drain on kitchen paper then serve hot, with nước chấm.

Serving Suggestion

Use a lettuce leaf to wrap a spring roll along with fresh herbs like mint, coriander (cilantro) and Thai basil, then dip generously in the nước chấm for the perfect bite. For a more substantial meal, cut the spring rolls into bite-sized pieces and serve with noodles, adding fresh herbs and pickles, then drizzle with a fish sauce dressing to create an incredible noodle salad bowl.

BÁNH MÌ BÒ NƯỚNG

CHILLI MARMALADE BRISKET BÁNH MÌ

TAKES 3 HOURS — SERVES 4

A bold and flavour-packed bánh mì, featuring tender, oven-baked brisket glazed with a spicy marmalade sauce. Balanced with tangy pickled vegetables, rich pâté and fresh herbs, this is the ultimate Vietnamese sandwich.

750g (1lb 10oz) beef brisket, excess fat trimmed
4 small baguettes, sliced open and middle crumb pulled out
150g (5oz) coarse pork pâté (or chicken or mushroom pâté)
40g (1½oz) daikon and carrot pickle (see page 180)
4 tsp mayonnaise
4 tsp sriracha sauce
5g (⅙oz) mint, leaves picked
5g (⅙oz) coriander (cilantro), leaves picked

FOR THE CHILLI MARMALADE
4 tbsp oyster sauce
1 tbsp fish sauce
2 tbsp marmalade
1 tbsp garlic granules
1 tbsp chilli powder
2 tbsp sesame oil

Preheat the oven to 130°C/110°C fan/260°F/Gas ½.

In a bowl, mix the chilli marmalade ingredients together well and rub evenly over the brisket.

Place the brisket in a deep roasting tray, cover tightly with foil and bake for 2½ hours until tender. Rest for 20 minutes, then slice thinly against the grain.

Warm the scooped-out baguettes and spread the pâté inside. Fill with the brisket, pickles, mayonnaise, sriracha and herbs, and serve immediately.

NEM NƯỚNG

GRILLED PORK SKEWERS

TAKES 30 MINUTES, PLUS MARINATING — MAKES 16

Nem nướng is a popular street food from southern Vietnam, known for its smoky, grilled flavour. Traditionally cooked over charcoal, this version uses an oven grill (broiler) for ease, without compromising on the rich, smoky taste or the delicious caramelization that comes from grilling. The skewered pork has a juicy, slightly crisp texture, making it a perfect choice for a main dish or as part of a larger Vietnamese meal.

You will need: 16 wooden or metal skewers (if using wooden ones, soak for 30 minutes before use)

500g (1lb 2oz) minced (ground) pork (20% fat)
2 garlic cloves, finely chopped
1 shallot, finely chopped
2 tbsp fish sauce
1 tbsp light soy sauce
1 tbsp brown sugar
1 tbsp condensed milk
2 tsp cornflour (cornstarch)
1 tsp coarsely ground black pepper
1 tsp five-spice powder
1 tbsp butter

In a large bowl, combine all the ingredients except the butter. Mix thoroughly until well combined. Leave it to marinate for at least 30 minutes, or overnight in the fridge for a richer flavour (removing from the fridge 30 minutes before cooking to bring to room temperature).

Take small portions of the mixture and mould each onto a skewer, forming a sausage-like shape. Press the mixture firmly onto the skewers to ensure they stay together during cooking.

Preheat the oven grill (broiler) to medium-high.

Lightly grease a baking tray with the butter. Arrange the skewers on the tray and grill (broil) for 6–8 minutes on each side, or until they are nicely browned and cooked through.

For a more traditional approach, cook the skewers in a frying pan (skillet) over a medium heat, or grill them on an outdoor barbecue (grill) for that authentic smoky flavour.

Serving Suggestion

Nem nướng skewers are a versatile dish: serve with rice paper, fresh herbs and lettuce for a classic wrap. Add pickled vegetables for a crunch and pair with steamed rice and a nước chấm dipping sauce. For a complete Vietnamese meal, complement with bánh xèo (savoury pancakes), or gỏi cuốn (fresh spring rolls).

THỊT BÒ LỤI SỐT ĐẬU PHỘNG

BEEF SKEWERS AND PEANUT SAUCE

TAKES 30 MINUTES, PLUS MARINATING — MAKES 16

Flame grilling is a very popular cooking method across Vietnam, celebrated for creating those irresistible charred flavours so iconic in street food. These beef skewers are a versatile favourite, perfect as part of a family meal or when served al fresco as street food. The smoky aroma and bold, punchy flavours make them a real standout dish for a barbecue (grill). I like to make them in batches and freeze the extra. Work once, enjoy twice (or more)!

You will need: 16 wooden or metal skewers (if using wooden ones, soak for 30 minutes before use)

500g (1lb 2oz) beef topside (top round), thinly sliced against the grain

FOR THE PEANUT SAUCE
3 tbsp crunchy peanut butter
1 tbsp hoisin sauce
1 tbsp light soy sauce
1 tbsp honey
50ml (3½ tbsp) hot water
Juice of 1 lime

FOR THE MARINADE
4 lemongrass stalks, finely chopped
6 shallots, finely chopped
200ml (7fl oz) all-purpose marinade (see page 181)

In a small bowl, mix together the peanut sauce ingredients until smooth. Set aside.

In a large bowl, mix the marinade ingredients together. Add the beef and toss well to coat. Leave to marinate for at least 30 minutes, or in the fridge for up to 3 hours, or even overnight for perfect results (removing from the fridge 30 minutes before cooking to bring to room temperature).

Thread the marinated beef onto the skewers, folding each slice concertina-style, in an 'S' shape.

Heat a cast iron griddle (grill) pan over a medium heat. Grill (broil) the skewers for 2–3 minutes on each side, until the beef is charred around the edges and the marinade is caramelizing.

Serve the skewers with the peanut sauce, either on the side for dipping, or drizzled over them.

Serving Suggestion
Traditionally served with vermicelli rice noodles or tucked into a bánh mì with fresh herbs and pickles, my favourite way is as here – just dunked in loads of peanut sauce! Or you could try switching up the dip with nước chấm (see page 175) or sweet soy sauce (see page 178). Both are equally addictive!

BÁNH BURGER CHẢ GIÒ

PORK AND PRAWN CHẢ GIÒ BURGER

TAKES 30 MINUTES — SERVES 4

If you're familiar with the flavours of Vietnamese spring rolls – chả giò – you'll know how irresistible that famous pork and prawn filling is. This turns it into a juicy patty. With crunchy water chestnuts, chewy mushrooms and the light, bouncy texture of prawns, each bite is packed with flavour and contrast, turning the humble burger into something truly special. Whether for a casual lunch or relaxed dinner, these chả giò burgers are sure to impress.

2 tbsp vegetable oil
4 brioche burger buns
60g (2oz) watercress
200g (7oz) daikon and carrot pickle (see page 180)

FOR THE PATTIES
50g (1¾oz) glass noodles
50g (1¾oz) dried shiitake mushrooms, soaked, then drained
100g (3½oz) drained, canned water chestnuts, finely chopped
200g (7oz) minced (ground) pork (20% fat)
300g (10½oz) raw king prawns (jumbo shrimp), peeled and deveined
4 spring onions (scallions), chopped
2 tbsp fish sauce
1 tbsp oyster sauce
1 tbsp garlic powder
1 tbsp golden caster (superfine) sugar
2 tbsp coarsely ground black pepper
4 egg yolks

FOR THE BURGER SAUCE
10g (⅓oz) coriander (cilantro)
10g (⅓oz) mint
4 tbsp mayonnaise
4 tbsp sriracha sauce
4 tbsp horseradish sauce
4 tbsp olive oil

For the patties, cook the noodles according to the packet instructions. Then pat dry the noodles, mushrooms and water chestnuts thoroughly using kitchen paper or a clean cloth – this is key to getting the right texture.

Add to a food processor along with the remaining patty ingredients and pulse until just combined, keeping it slightly chunky for that signature spring roll texture. Shape into 4 patties and set aside.

For the burger sauce, finely chop the coriander stalks and leaves and the mint leaves. Combine all the burger sauce ingredients in a small bowl. Set aside.

Heat the oil in a large frying pan (skillet) over a medium heat. Fry the patties for 5–6 minutes on each side, until golden and cooked through. Meanwhile, split and toast the burger buns.

To assemble the burgers, spread burger sauce on both bun halves. Add the cooked patty to the bottom bun, then layer with the watercress and pickles. Top with the remaining bun halves and serve immediately.

Serving Suggestion
Serve with a side of crispy sweet potato fries or, for a lighter option, a fresh green salad.

THỊT HEO NƯỚNG TACOS

HONEY AND CHILLI PORK TACOS

TAKES 1 HOUR, PLUS MARINATING — MAKES 8

This dish is my way of bringing vibrant Vietnamese flavours to the humble taco. Patience is key while the pork marinates, but the first bite makes it all worthwhile. It really highlights what I love about Vietnamese cooking; simple appearances often hide the care and effort that go into every detail. Hours of preparation, minutes of enjoyment – but memories that last long after.

500g (1lb 2oz) pork tenderloin
1 tbsp vegetable oil
3 tbsp runny honey
8 soft tortillas
400g (14oz) daikon and carrot pickle (see page 180)
1 red onion, thinly sliced
5g (⅙oz) Thai basil, leaves picked
5g (⅙oz) coriander (cilantro), leaves picked
10 French radishes, thinly sliced
8 tsp garlic mayo
8 tsp chilli sauce
8 pinches of coarsely ground black pepper
3 red chillies, thinly sliced
8 pinches of crispy fried shallots (see page 180 for homemade)

FOR THE MARINADE
5 tbsp all-purpose marinade (see page 181)
3 tbsp hoisin sauce
1 tsp five-spice powder
2 tsp paprika

In a bowl, combine all the marinade ingredients. Add the pork tenderloin and rub the marinade into the meat evenly, ensuring it's thoroughly coated. Cover and marinate for at least 3 hours or ideally overnight in the fridge for best results (removing from the fridge 30 minutes before cooking to bring to room temperature).

Preheat the oven to 180°C/160°C fan/350°F/Gas 4.

Heat the vegetable oil in an ovenproof frying pan (skillet) or skillet and sear the pork fillet evenly until caramelized. Transfer to the oven and roast for 30 minutes, brushing the pork with honey every 10 minutes to develop flavour and colour.

Remove from the oven and leave the pork to rest for 8–10 minutes before slicing thinly.

Warm the tortillas and layer with slices of the pork, pickles, red onion, Thai basil, coriander, radish, garlic mayo and chilli sauce. Sprinkle with black pepper and finish with chillies and crispy fried shallots, for that delightful crunch.

BÁNH GẠO HẢI SẢN

SEAFOOD RICE CRACKERS

TAKES 20 MINUTES — SERVES 4

When a dish is as fun to make as it is to eat, it's a win in my household. This simple recipe is a great way to get the kids involved, and the result is a platter of crispy, flavour-packed bites that steal the show at any party. Light, crunchy and full of seafood goodness, these rice crackers are the ultimate nibble for any feast.

10 square Vietnamese rice papers
140g (5oz) cooked, peeled king prawns (jumbo shrimp)
25g (1oz) chives, finely chopped
250g (9oz) crab sticks
Vegetable oil, for frying
200ml (7fl oz) nước chấm (see page 175), sweet chilli sauce or chilli mayo

To prepare the rice papers, fill a large bowl with cold water, then use a clean J-cloth (food cloth) to wipe water across both sides of one rice paper.

Place 6 prawns on the rice paper, evenly spaced. Sprinkle with chives and cover with a second moistened sheet.

Leave for 15–20 seconds, then press the rice paper together with your fingers to seal, before cutting into 6 rectangular pieces.

Repeat the process with the remaining prawns, then with the crab sticks to make the rest.

Pour in enough oil to a deep frying pan, to a depth of 5cm (2 inch), and heat to 180°C (356°F). To check if the oil is ready, dip a wooden chopstick into it; if bubbles form around the chopstick, it's ready.

Fry each piece individually for a few seconds, until white/opaque and crisp.

Serve with a classic nước chấm (or sweet chilli sauce or chilli mayo), for an extra kick.

BÒ NÉ

THE 'FULL VIETNAMESE' BREAKFAST

TAKES 20 MINUTES, PLUS MARINATING — SERVES 1

The full Vietnamese breakfast is my take on the classic steak and eggs, offering a sizzling, flavour-packed start to the day. Served on a hot pan with tender beef, runny eggs and fresh vegetables, it's paired with a crispy baguette to soak up all those delicious juices. The perfect way to start your weekend!

This dish is one I enjoy very much, but I love the name even more. In Vietnam, dishes are often given quite literal names, and this is one of my favourites. Bò means beef, and né means 'to dodge'. It is served sizzling on a cast iron plate, spitting hot oil as it arrives at the table. Your natural reaction is to dodge, and so the name was born.

400g (14oz) beef rib-eye steak, cut into thin strips
200ml (7fl oz) all-purpose marinade (see page 181)
1 tbsp vegetable oil
12 cherry tomatoes on the vine
2 eggs
1 tbsp coarse pâté (such as chicken liver, pork, or pork and chicken)
30g (1oz) butter, plus extra for the bread
1 spring onion (scallion), sliced
3 sprigs of coriander (cilantro)
2 pinches of coarsely ground black pepper

TO SERVE
15g (½oz) daikon and carrot pickle (see page 180)
2 tsp chilli oil or chilli sauce (or both)
¼ cucumber, sliced
1 small baguette

In a bowl, mix the steak with the all-purpose marinade, ensuring a full and even coating. Leave to marinate for at least 10 minutes, or up to 3 hours in the fridge if you have the time (removing from the fridge 30 minutes before cooking to bring to room temperature).

Heat a large cast iron griddle (grill) pan over a medium-high heat. Add the vegetable oil and, when hot, add the marinated steak and sear for 1–2 minutes; we just want a char. Remove from the pan and add in the tomatoes. Cook for 3–4 minutes until slightly blistered, then push to one side of the pan.

Crack the eggs into the pan and cook them sunny-side up (or your preferred way). Add the pâté to the pan, allowing it to melt slightly. Return the steak to the pan, arranging it alongside the eggs and vegetables.

Add the butter to the pan, then garnish with the spring onion, coriander and black pepper. Serve the sizzling dish directly from the pan with the pickles and a drizzle of chilli oil or sauce, and a side of cucumber slices with a crusty baguette spread with the butter.

Serving Suggestion
Enjoy this full Vietnamese breakfast with a strong cup of Vietnamese coffee, for the ultimate start to your day.

BÁNH KHOÁI

THE JOY PANCAKE

TAKES 30 MINUTES — SERVES 4

There's something both endearing and confident about a dish named after the feeling it gives you. Bánh khoái means 'delight' or 'joy' cake. This crispy, savoury pancake originates from Huế, the historic capital of Vietnam's central region. Traditionally served with a rich hoisin dipping sauce, this version swaps that out for a lighter nước chấm with sesame seeds. My take stays true to the spirit of the dish, preserving its joyful texture and bold, satisfying flavours, while using more accessible ingredients.

8 tbsp vegetable oil
4 eggs, beaten
280g (10oz) cooked and peeled king prawns (jumbo shrimp)
4 spring onions (scallions), finely chopped
200g (7oz) beansprouts
4 tsp crispy fried shallots (see page 180 for homemade), to garnish

FOR THE BATTER
100g (3½oz) rice flour
25g (1oz) plain (all-purpose) flour
½ tsp salt
1 tsp sugar
½ tsp baking powder
1 tsp ground turmeric
300ml (10fl oz/1¼ cups) coconut cream (NOT milk)

FOR THE SESAME NƯỚC CHẤM
2 tsp white sesame seeds
400ml (14fl oz/1¾ cups) nước chấm (page 175)

FOR THE SALAD
½ fresh pineapple, peeled and cored
1 star fruit or green (unripe) mango
2 baby gem lettuce
80g (3oz) pea shoots
120g (4oz) rocket (arugula)
25g (1oz) Thai basil
25g (1oz) purple perilla (page 140)

In a large bowl, whisk together all the batter ingredients until smooth.

In a small bowl, stir the sesame seeds into the nước chấm and set aside.

Heat a 20cm (8 inch) cast iron skillet or non-stick frying pan (skillet) over a medium heat. Add 2 tablespoons of oil and, when hot, pour in about 75ml (5 tbsp) batter, swirling the pan to coat the base evenly.

Drizzle over 1 tbsp of beaten egg, then sprinkle over some prawns, spring onion and beansprouts (if you like them softened; if not, save them for the salad). Cook for around 2 minutes, until the base is crisp and golden.

Fold the pancake in half to enclose the filling, and transfer to a plate. Repeat with the remaining batter and fillings to make 4 pancakes.

Slice the pineapple and star fruit or mango. Arrange the salad platter in the centre of the table and garnish with crispy fried shallots.

To eat, wrap pieces of pancake in lettuce with herbs and fruit, dip into the sesame nước chấm, and enjoy every joyful bite.

Make it Veggie
Just as joyful but without the prawns! Swap them for smoked or marinated tofu, and serve with sweet soy sauce (see page 178) for dipping.

Light Bites and Starters

BÁNH HOÀNH THÁNH TÔM

PRAWN AND CHIVE DIAMOND DUMPLINGS

TAKES 45 MINUTES — SERVES 6 (MAKES 34–40)

What's not to love about these tasty parcels, especially when served with a classic nước chấm dipping sauce? I love making them with friends and family as it turns meal prep into a social experience that's both fun and productive, sparking plenty of conversation. These versatile dumplings work as a main course, appetizer, or when added to soups or noodles. You can easily switch up the filling or even make them vegetarian. They also freeze beautifully – perfect for those rainy days when you need a quick, comforting meal.

4 eggs, separated
About 40 wonton wrappers

FOR THE FILLING
100g (3½oz) minced (ground) chicken
400g (14oz) raw king prawns (jumbo shrimp), peeled and deveined
25g (1oz) chives, finely chopped
1 tbsp fish sauce
1 tbsp light soy sauce
1 tbsp sesame oil
1 chicken stock (bouillon) cube, crumbled
2 tsp coarsely ground black pepper
1 tbsp garlic powder

TO FINISH AND SERVE
200ml (7fl oz) nước chấm (see page 175)
6 tsp ginger and chive oil (see page 179)
6 tsp chilli and lemongrass oil (see page 179)
20g (¾oz) crispy fried shallots (see page 180 for homemade)

In a food processor, pulse all the filling ingredients with the egg yolks until well combined, keeping the prawns slightly chunky for texture.

Place a wonton wrapper in your palm with a corner pointing towards you (like a diamond). Add a heaped teaspoon of the filling to the centre. Lightly brush the edges with egg white. Fold the bottom corner up to meet the top, forming a triangle. Press around the filling to seal tightly, pushing out any air. With the long edge of the triangle facing you, bring the two side corners together so they slightly overlap. Dab one corner with egg white, pinch the two ends together and press to seal, forming a diamond, or boat, shape. Repeat with remaining wrappers and filling.

To cook, lower into a pan of boiling water and cook for 7–8 minutes, or steam for 10–12 minutes, until cooked through.

To serve, spoon over nước chấm, drizzle with ginger and chive oil and chilli and lemongrass oil, then finish with a generous sprinkle of crispy fried shallots.

Make it Veggie
Swap the chicken and prawns out for the same weight in tofu.

Light Bites and Starters

BÁNH TRỨNG NƯỚNG VỚI THỊT XÔNG KHÓI VÀ TÔM

BACON AND PRAWN QUICHE

TAKES 1 HOUR — SERVES 6

This dish combines two favourites: the classic Vietnamese pork meatloaf topped with steamed egg (chả trứng hấp) and the French quiche. Vietnamese chả trứng is traditionally served alongside grilled pork chops, pickles and fresh herbs – often seen as just a sidekick. But for me, it was always the best part. So here, I'm making it the star of the show! It brings a rich, savoury base while the quiche adds creamy indulgence. Together, they create a fusion perfect for brunch or a light dinner.

1 sheet of ready-rolled shortcrust (pie crust) pastry
1 tbsp vegetable oil
100g (3½oz) bacon lardons
140g (5oz) cooked tiger prawns (shrimp), chopped
1 echalion shallot, chopped
50g (1¾oz) shiitake mushrooms (or dry fungus mushrooms)
3 garlic cloves, chopped
50g (1¾oz) glass noodles, cooked according to the packet instructions, then chopped
1 tsp fish sauce
1 tsp coarsely ground black pepper
3 spring onions (scallions), chopped
10g (⅓oz) coriander (cilantro), stalks and leaves chopped
6 eggs
300ml (10fl oz/1¼ cups) crème fraîche
300ml (10fl oz/1¼ cups) double (heavy) cream
100g (3½oz) Gruyère cheese, grated

Preheat the oven to 200°C/180°C fan/400°F/Gas 6.

Use the pastry to line a 22cm (8½ inch) non-stick loose-bottom tart or quiche tin (pan). Trim any excess and crimp the edges. Line with baking parchment, fill with ceramic baking beans and blind bake for 10 minutes. Remove and set aside. Reduce the oven temperature to 180°C/160°C fan/350°F/Gas 4.

In a large pan, heat the oil over a high heat. Add the lardons, prawns, shallot, mushrooms and garlic. Sauté for 3–4 minutes until lightly browned but not crispy. Take off the heat and stir in the chopped noodles, fish sauce, black pepper, spring onions and coriander. Mix evenly.

In a large bowl, lightly beat 4 of the eggs then whisk together with the crème fraîche and double cream. Fold in the filling mixture and Gruyère and combine well. Separate the remaining eggs, reserving only the yolks.

Pour the mixture into the pre-baked pastry case and bake for 30–35 minutes until the filling is just set and golden. Five minutes before the end of the cooking time, remove from the oven, brush with the reserved egg yolks and return for the final 5 minutes. Allow to cool for a few minutes before slicing.

Serving Suggestion

This quiche is delicious hot or at room temperature. Serve with a light green salad and a tangy vinaigrette. For a Vietnamese twist, pair with đồ chua (pickled vegetables) or a simple cucumber and tomato salad.

Light Bites and Starters

TÀU HỦ SẢ TẾ GỪNG

GINGER SILKEN TOFU

TAKES 10 MINUTES — SERVES 1–2

A light yet flavourful dish that shows how simple ingredients can create bold, fragrant flavours. Tofu is often unfairly criticized for being bland, but I see it differently. Think of tofu, especially silken, as a blank canvas. Its delicate flavour and texture are the perfect vessel to soak up all the beautiful ingredients you introduce to the dish. It's not designed to bring the flavour; it's there to carry it.

In Vietnam, silken tofu is best known as a comforting warm dessert, served with a rich ginger caramel syrup. Here, I'm sharing a savoury version, but one where ginger still holds the spotlight. If it's your first time trying silken tofu, I promise it won't be your last.

350g (12oz) silken tofu
3 tbsp chilli and lemongrass oil (see page 179)
2 tbsp ginger and chive oil (see page 179)
2 tbsp light soy sauce
1 tbsp golden caster (superfine) sugar
20g (¾oz) ginger, peeled and julienned
5 sprigs of coriander (cilantro), stems chopped, leaves picked

Carefully transfer the silken tofu to a serving plate.

In a small saucepan over a low heat, combine the chilli and lemongrass oil, ginger and chive oil, soy sauce and sugar. Stir for 1–2 minutes until the sugar has fully dissolved.

Pour the warm dressing over the tofu. Sprinkle with julienned ginger and finish with coriander.

Serving Suggestion

This is delicious on its own and large enough to make a satisfying yet light lunch. Or to turn it into a wholesome family meal, pair it with steamed rice, vegetables and meat dishes of your choice.

Light Bites and Starters

SOUPS AND NOODLES

SÚP HÀNH PHỞ

BEEF FILLET PHỞ SOUP

TAKES: 45 MINUTES — SERVES 4

The French influence on Vietnamese cuisine is undeniable, with dishes like bánh mì and phở showcasing French techniques and ingredients. This recipe takes that fusion a step further, reimagining the classic French onion soup with bold Vietnamese flavours. The caramelized onions and rich broth of French onion soup meet the fragrant spices and delicate beef fillet of Vietnamese phở, creating a new and delicious cross-cultural dish.

400g (14oz) beef fillet
1 tsp salt
1 tbsp vegetable oil
1 tbsp butter
4 onions, thinly sliced
2 shallots, thinly sliced
3 garlic cloves, finely chopped
3 lemongrass stalks, halved and crushed
10 star anise
10g (⅓oz) cinnamon stick
2 litres (4¼ pints) beef stock (broth)
2 tbsp fish sauce
2 tsp sugar
2 beef stock (bouillon) cubes, crumbled
1 tsp coarsely ground black pepper, plus extra to garnish

TO GARNISH AND SERVE
4 sprigs of coriander (cilantro)
4 sprigs of Thai basil
4 mini baguettes, halved crossways, toasted and buttered

Lightly salt the beef, rubbing it into all sides of the fillet.

Heat the vegetable oil in a medium frying pan or griddle (grill) pan over a high heat. Sear the fillet for 30 seconds on each side, until just browned, then remove from the pan. Set aside.

In the same pan, melt the butter over a medium heat. Add the onions, shallots, garlic and lemongrass and cook for 20–25 minutes, stirring occasionally, until they become deeply golden and caramelized.

Stir in the star anise and cinnamon stick, then pour in the stock, along with the fish sauce, sugar, stock cubes and black pepper. Bring to a simmer and leave to cook for 10–15 minutes, allowing the flavours to fully infuse. Remove the whole spices.

Slice the beef as thinly as possible then ladle the hot soup into 4 bowls. Lay slices of the thin beef on top, allowing the heat of the soup to lightly cook the meat.

Garnish with the coriander, Thai basil and black pepper, and serve each with a toasted buttered baguette.

MÌ HẢI SẢN

PORK AND SEAFOOD NOODLE SOUP

TAKES 30 MINUTES — SERVES 2

Inspired by the traditional southern Vietnamese broth, hủ tiếu, this noodle soup has a wonderfully delicate, flavourful broth. It's the perfect base for tasty toppings like pork, prawns and squid. I love this combination, and especially enjoy the twist that the heavier, bolder-flavoured egg noodles bring to the dish.

2 tbsp vegetable oil, plus extra
150g (5oz) minced (ground) pork
1 tsp garlic powder
2 tsp salt
6 cooked, peeled tiger prawns (shrimp)
150g (5oz) cooked squid rings
1 red chicory (endive), halved lengthways
3 echalion shallots, halved lengthways
6 fresh lime leaves
5g (⅛oz) ginger, sliced and crushed
1.2 litres (2½ pints) chicken stock (broth)
2 chicken stock (bouillon) cubes
30g (1oz) rock sugar
2 tbsp fish sauce

TO SERVE
200g (7oz) egg noodles
6 quail's eggs, hard-boiled for 4 minutes, then peeled
4 sprigs of Asian (or regular) chives
5g (⅛oz) coriander (cilantro), leaves roughly torn
1 lime, cut into wedges
2 tbsp chilli and lemongrass oil (see page 179)
1 tsp coarsely ground black pepper

Cook the noodles according to the packet instructions.

Heat 1 tablespoon of the vegetable oil in a pot and add the pork. Season with the garlic powder and 1 teaspoon of the salt. Fry for 2–3 minutes until light brown, breaking it up with a wooden spoon as it cooks, then remove and set aside.

Add a little more oil to the pot if needed. Add the cooked prawns and squid and the red chicory and warm through for 1 minute. Set aside with the pork.

Wipe the pot, then heat the remaining tablespoon of oil. Add the shallots, lime leaves and ginger and cook for 3 minutes until browned.

Add the chicken stock, crumble in the stock cubes, then add the sugar and remaining salt. Bring to the boil, skim off any impurities, then simmer over a medium heat for 20 minutes.

Remove the ginger, lime leaves and shallots and finish with the fish sauce – this preserves its umami punch.

Divide the noodles between 2 bowls. Top with the pork, prawns, squid, quail's eggs, chicory and chives. Ladle over the hot broth, then garnish with the coriander, lime wedges and chilli and lemongrass oil and sprinkle over the black pepper.

PHỞ VỊT QUAY

ROAST DUCK NOODLE SOUP

TAKES 1 HOUR — SERVES 4

Wondering what to make next after the Vietnamese roast duck (see page 117)? This comforting noodle soup was made for that moment. A leftover roast duck carcass will never go to waste again! This recipe is proof of how easily rich, comforting flavours can be extracted from the simplest ingredients. Growing up, nothing was ever wasted in our home. Every part of an ingredient served a purpose, and I truly believe that this mindset sparks creativity, often leading to the best 'accidental' recipes. Some of these, over time, even become tradition. But, if you only have the meat and no carcass, simply swap the water for duck or chicken stock; both work beautifully!

1 tbsp vegetable oil
100g (3½oz) ginger, sliced and crushed
2 lemongrass stalks, crushed
5 echalion shallots, halved lengthways
20g (¾oz) star anise
20g (¾oz) cinnamon stick
8 fresh lime leaves
1 whole roast duck carcass, plus leftover roast duck meat, shredded
1 white cabbage, chopped into large chunks
5 carrots, halved
2.5 litres (5¼ pints) water
2 tsp sea salt
50g (1¾oz) rock sugar
70ml (2½fl oz) fish sauce
4 tbsp duck fat
4 spring onions (scallions)

TO FINISH AND SERVE
400g (14oz) vermicelli rice noodles
1 lime, halved
10g (⅓oz) coriander (cilantro)
10g (⅓oz) dill
4 tbsp hoisin sauce
Fresh chillies or chilli oil (optional)

Heat the vegetable oil in a large, 8-litre (8½ quart) stockpot. Add the ginger, lemongrass and shallots, charring them for 5 minutes each side. Add the star anise, cinnamon and lime leaves, cooking for a further 2 minutes.

Add the duck carcass (reserving the meat), cabbage and carrots. Pour in the water and bring to the boil, skimming off any impurities, then reduce the heat to medium-low and simmer, partially covered, for 45 minutes.

Strain the broth, discarding the solids, then return the broth to the pot and add the salt, sugar, fish sauce and duck fat. Cut the spring onions in half and add them too. Bring back to the boil just before serving.

Meanwhile, cook, drain and rinse the rice noodles, then divide between 4 bowls. Add the shredded roast duck and ladle over the hot broth. Finish with a squeeze of lime and a sprinkle of herbs, then serve with the hoisin sauce and optional chilli on the side.

MIẾN GÀ

CHICKEN GLASS NOODLE SOUP

TAKES 30 MINUTES, PLUS MARINATING — SERVES 4

Miến gà is a lighter, more delicate broth than the better-known phở gà, yet just as full of flavour. Without the use of heavy spices, the broth remains subtle and refined, allowing the natural clarity to shine. This dish celebrates simplicity: silky, bouncy glass noodles, tender chicken breast, and a clean, comforting broth that soothes with every spoonful. You can easily swap the chicken for pork, salmon or tiger prawns.

3 tsp salt
2 corn-fed (for the colour) boneless, skin-on chicken breasts
About 2 tbsp vegetable oil
100g (3½oz) ginger, peeled and crushed
2 onions, halved
2 litres (4¼ pints) chicken stock (broth)
4 tbsp fish sauce
30g (1oz) rock sugar
2 chicken stock (bouillon) cubes, crumbled

TO FINISH AND SERVE
200g (7oz) mung bean glass noodles, cooked according to the packet instructions
40g (1½oz) beansprouts
20g (¾oz) coriander (cilantro), stalks and leaves chopped
2 tsp coarsely ground black pepper
4 tsp crispy fried shallots (see page 180 for homemade)
1 lime, quartered
2 red chillies, sliced
4 spring onions, finely chopped

Rub 2 teaspoons of the salt onto the skin of the chicken breasts. Add 2 tablespoons of vegetable oil to a large pot over a medium heat. Place the chicken skin-side down in the oil and cook for 8–10 minutes until golden and crisp. Flip and cook for a further 12–15 minutes, or until fully cooked (internal temperature of 74°C/165°F). Remove and set aside to cool, then slice against the grain into pieces 2cm (¾ inch) thick.

Add a little more oil to the pot, if needed. Increase the heat to high and add the ginger and onions. Sear for 4–5 minutes until lightly charred.

Pour in the chicken stock and bring to the boil. Add the fish sauce, sugar, remaining salt and crumbled stock cubes. Skim off any impurities, then reduce to a simmer while you prepare the bowls.

To serve, place a portion of cooked glass noodles into each bowl. Add beansprouts as a base, followed by the sliced chicken on top. Ladle over the hot broth.

Garnish with coriander, a pinch of black pepper and crispy fried shallots. Serve with lime wedges and sliced chillies on the side, and sprinkle with the spring onion.

Make it Veggie
Swap the chicken for tofu, adjusting the seasoning with salt or soy sauce instead of fish sauce, and use veg stock and stock cubes.

BÚN HUẾ CHAY

TOFU HUẾ-STYLE NOODLE SOUP

TAKES 15 MINUTES — SERVES 4

My simple and delicious take on the iconic bún bò Huế, a spicy noodle soup from Vietnam's former imperial city of Huế. While the traditional version uses beef, this plant-based twist holds its own with a deeply aromatic broth infused with lemongrass, ginger and chilli. It's bold, comforting and wonderfully fragrant, perfect for any time of year. Try swapping the noodles, too – a small change that brings a fresh take to the dish!

2 tsp vegetable oil
3 lemongrass stalks, halved and crushed
50g (1¾oz) ginger, sliced and crushed
6 fresh lime leaves
500ml (17fl oz/generous 2 cups) vegetable stock (broth)
1 tbsp umami paste
30g (1oz) rock sugar
1 tsp salt
4 tbsp chilli and lemongrass oil (see page 179)
200g (7oz) silken tofu, cut into 3cm (1¼ inch) cubes
200g (7oz) shiitake mushrooms
400g (14oz) udon noodles or mung bean noodles

TO GARNISH AND SERVE
5g (⅙oz) coriander (cilantro) leaves
5g (⅙oz) Thai basil leaves
2 spring onions (scallions), finely sliced
1 lime, cut into wedges
2 red chillies, finely sliced

Heat the vegetable oil in a large pot over a high heat. Add the lemongrass, ginger and lime leaves and sauté for 2 minutes until a little browned and fragrant.

Pour in the vegetable stock, stir in the umami paste, sugar, salt and chilli and lemongrass oil.

Add the tofu and mushrooms, bring to a gentle boil, then lower the heat and simmer for 10 minutes.

Meanwhile, cook the noodles according to the packet instructions and divide them between 4 serving bowls.

Ladle the hot broth over the noodles, ensuring each bowl gets plenty of tofu and mushrooms. Garnish with the coriander, Thai basil and spring onions. Serve with lime wedges and chilli slices on the side.

BÚN RIÊU CHAY

KING OYSTER MUSHROOM AND TOMATO NOODLE SOUP

TAKES 30 MINUTES — SERVES 4

Bún riêu chay is a plant-based twist on the beloved northern Vietnamese tomato and crab noodle soup, bún riêu. Traditionally made with pork and freshwater crab, this version celebrates the same tangy, comforting broth using vibrant tomatoes and meaty king oyster mushrooms. Often served during Buddhist fasting periods, this dish is light yet deeply satisfying – a true taste of Vietnamese street food, minus the meat.

200g (3½oz) tofu, half mashed with a fork and half cut into matchsticks
3 eggs, lightly beaten
2 tbsp vegetable oil
200g (7oz) king oyster mushrooms, sliced
2 echalion shallots, chopped
4 garlic cloves, chopped
24 cherry tomatoes
1.5 litres (3¼ pints/6 cups) vegetable stock (broth)
4 tbsp tomato purée (paste)
1 tsp paprika
1 tbsp umami paste
1 tsp sugar
1 tsp salt, or to taste
400g (14oz) vermicelli rice noodles, cooked according to the packet instructions

TO GARNISH AND SERVE
5g (⅙oz) Thai basil, leaves picked
5g (⅙oz) coriander (cilantro), leaves chopped
25g (1oz) chives, chopped
4 tsp crispy fried shallots (see page 180 for homemade)
1 lime, cut into wedges
2 red chillies, sliced

In a small bowl, mix the mashed tofu and eggs together. Set aside.

Heat 1 tablespoon of the vegetable oil in a large pot over a high heat. Sear the mushrooms on one side only for 2 minutes until charred. Remove and set aside.

Add the remaining oil to the pot. Sauté the shallots, garlic and cherry tomatoes for 2 minutes until browned. Pour in the stock and bring to the boil. Stir in the tomato purée, paprika, umami paste, sugar and salt.

Add the tofu matchsticks, then gently pour in the tofu-egg mixture. Lower the heat and cook for 6–7 minutes until the cherry tomatoes soften and the tofu-egg mix sets. Use a spoon to break it into 4 rustic chunks.

Divide the noodles between 4 bowls. Add the mushrooms, tofu matchsticks, tomatoes and tofu-egg chunks. Ladle the hot broth over everything – it should be piping hot when served.

Garnish with the Thai basil, coriander, chives and crispy fried shallots, and serve with lime wedges and chilli slices on the side.

BÁNH CANH CUA CÁ HỒI UDON

SEAFOOD AND COCONUT UDON

TAKES 30 MINUTES — SERVES 2

This creamy, indulgent soup brings together rich umami flavours and a delightful mix of textures. Drawing inspiration from a childhood favourite of mine, bánh canh cua nước cốt dừa, this dish showcases bouncy udon noodles soaking up a delicious coconut broth, enhanced by fresh herbs for an aromatic finish.

2 tsp vegetable oil
160g (5½oz) hot-smoked salmon, warmed
50g (1¾oz) cooked squid rings, warmed
300ml (10fl oz/1¼ cups) chicken stock (broth)
400ml (14fl oz) coconut milk
100ml (3½fl oz) water
200g (7oz) mixed crab meat
2 tsp paprika
½ tsp ground turmeric
2 chicken stock (bouillon) cubes, crumbled
1 tsp sugar
1 tsp fish sauce
100g (3½oz) udon noodles
1 tsp cornflour (cornstarch), dissolved in 5 tsp cold water

TO GARNISH AND SERVE
5g (⅛oz) kimchi
5g (⅛oz) chives, chopped
2 coriander (cilantro) stems, leaves picked
2 tsp crispy fried shallots (see page 180 for homemade)
2 tsp chilli oil (optional)

Heat the vegetable oil in a small pan over a medium heat. Add the smoked salmon and calamari and gently toss for 1–2 minutes until warmed, then set aside.

For the soup, in a saucepan, bring the chicken stock, coconut milk and water to the boil. Add the crab, paprika, turmeric, stock cubes, sugar and fish sauce, then lower the heat to medium and cook for 2 minutes.

Add the udon noodles and cook for 3–5 minutes until the noodles are soft and bouncy. Stir in the cornflour mixture and remove from the heat.

Divide the soup and noodles between 2 serving bowls. Top with the warm seafood and garnish with the kimchi, chives, coriander and crispy fried shallots, finishing with a drizzle of chilli oil for extra kick, if desired.

CANH BÍ CỐT DỪA

BUTTERNUT SQUASH AND COCONUT SOUP

TAKES 45 MINUTES — SERVES 4

This classic Vietnamese soup offers a warming blend of flavours, traditionally made with pumpkin but just as delicious with the more readily available butternut squash. Originating from southern Vietnam, it's enjoyed for its smooth texture and natural sweetness, thanks to the rich and creamy coconut. Often eaten as a vegetarian option during Buddhist holidays, this simple yet flavoursome dish captures the essence of Vietnamese home cooking.

1 tbsp vegetable oil
1 onion, finely chopped
2 garlic cloves, finely chopped
500g (1lb 2oz) butternut squash, peeled and cut into bite-sized pieces
500ml (17fl oz/generous 2 cups) vegetable stock (broth)
2 tbsp light soy sauce
1 tbsp golden caster (superfine) sugar
1 tbsp umami paste (ensure vegan, if necessary)
200ml (7fl oz) coconut milk
300ml (10fl oz/1¼ cups) coconut cream
1 tsp salt, to taste

TO GARNISH

5g (⅙oz) coriander (cilantro), leaves picked
4 pinches of coarsely ground black pepper
4 pinches of crispy fried shallots (see page 180 for homemade)

In a large pot, heat the vegetable oil over a medium heat. Once hot, add the onion and garlic and sauté for 2–3 minutes until lightly browned.

Add the cubed butternut squash and stir well for 2 minutes, allowing it to absorb all the flavours of the garlic and onion.

Add the stock, soy sauce, sugar and umami paste. Bring to the boil, then reduce the heat to low and simmer for 15 minutes. Stir in the coconut milk and cream and simmer for another 5–10 minutes, until the squash is tender. To finish off, season with salt to taste.

To serve, ladle the soup into bowls and garnish with the coriander, black pepper and crispy fried shallots.

Serving Suggestion

This soup is vegan but if you don't need it to be, or are not keen on coconut cream, then you can use extra-thick double (heavy) cream in its place. The soup is perfect served with steamed rice and a simple stir-fried vegetable dish, creating a tasty, healthy and balanced meal. Alternatively, it works wonderfully as a substantial vegetable side dish in a non-vegetarian meal.

MỲ Ý SỐT BOLOGNESE

SPAGHETTI BOLOGNESE

TAKES 45 MINUTES — SERVES 4

Spaghetti bolognese, an Italian classic and now an English staple, is known for its rich, indulgent flavours. Over time, I've naturally developed a Vietnamese-inspired version using ingredients from my pantry, and it's fast become a firm family favourite. Now I'm excited to share my fusion of Italian tradition and Vietnamese flavours with you!

1 tbsp vegetable oil
250g (9oz) minced (ground) beef
8 shallots, finely chopped
4 garlic cloves, finely chopped
2 lemongrass stalks, finely chopped
1 carrot, finely chopped
1 tbsp light soy sauce
1 tbsp fish sauce
1 tsp sugar
1 tsp coarsely ground black pepper
200g (7oz) cherry tomatoes, halved
200g (7oz) sun-dried tomatoes, chopped
3 tbsp tomato purée (paste)
200ml (7fl oz) beef stock (broth)
4 fresh lime leaves, thinly sliced
250g (9oz) spaghetti, cooked until al dente, then drained
1 tbsp sesame oil

TO SERVE
30g (1oz) Parmesan cheese, grated
5g (⅙oz) Thai basil, leaves picked

Heat the vegetable oil in a large pan over a medium heat. Add the beef and cook for 6–8 minutes until browned, breaking it up with a wooden spoon as it cooks.

Add the shallots, garlic and lemongrass to the pan and cook for a further 5 minutes, stirring occasionally, until the shallots become a golden colour.

Stir in the carrot, soy sauce, fish sauce, sugar and black pepper, then cook for another 2 minutes.

Add in the cherry tomatoes, sun-dried tomatoes, tomato purée and beef stock. Then mix in the lime leaves and bring to a simmer. Cook for 15 minutes, allowing the sauce to thicken and the flavours to infuse.

Add the cooked spaghetti to the pan, stirring to combine with the sauce. Cook for 2–3 more minutes until the spaghetti is well coated and heated through, then finish by drizzling over the sesame oil.

Serve topped with grated Parmesan and Thai basil.

Serving Suggestion

For an extra Vietnamese twist, add fresh chillies or a drizzle of chilli oil on top.

MIẾN KHOAI XÀO TỎI VỚI ĐẬU HŨ

SMOKED TOFU GARLIC-TOSSED SWEET POTATO VERMICELLI

TAKES 10 MINUTES — SERVES 4

A filling yet light option for those days when you want something easy, healthy and subtle in flavour. This quick combo hits all the right notes – smoky tofu, punchy chilli and lemongrass oil and chewy sweet potato noodles. Feel free to swap out the tofu for whatever protein you fancy. It's all about keeping it simple and delicious, so you can sit back and savour every bite.

2 tbsp vegetable oil

200g (7oz) smoked tofu, cut into matchsticks

4 garlic cloves, chopped

400g (14oz) sweet potato vermicelli noodles, cooked according to the packet instructions

4 tbsp chilli and lemongrass oil (see page 179)

4 tbsp light soy sauce

4 spring onions (scallions), sliced

4 tsp crispy fried shallots (see page 180 for homemade), to garnish

Heat 1 tablespoon of the vegetable oil in a frying pan (skillet) over a high heat. Add the tofu and toss for 2 minutes until lightly golden. Remove and set aside.

Add the remaining oil to the pan, then add the garlic and immediately toss in the cooked noodles. Stir through the chilli and lemongrass oil and soy sauce and cook for 2–3 minutes until warmed through and well coated.

Return the tofu to the pan along with the spring onions. Toss to combine evenly. Garnish with crispy fried shallots for that perfect crunch.

MÌ XÀO TỎI & LẠP XƯỞNG

GARLIC & LẠP XƯỞNG EGG NOODLES

TAKES 25 MINUTES — SERVES 2

This simple recipe is a great option for a family meal. The Vietnamese lạp xưởng sausages bring bold, distinctive flavours to the dish, while the garlic and Thai basil give it a fresh, aromatic touch. Topped with a perfectly runny egg, it strikes a satisfying balance between familiar and exciting.

- 250g (9oz) fresh egg noodles, cooked according to the packet instructions
- 4 Vietnamese lạp xưởng sausages, sliced (or 130g/4½oz chorizo, sliced)
- 1 tbsp vegetable oil, plus 2 tsp for the eggs
- 4 garlic cloves, finely chopped
- 2 lemongrass stalks, finely chopped
- 2 tbsp soy sauce
- 1 tbsp fish sauce
- 1 tbsp sesame oil
- 1 tsp sugar
- 2 spring onions (scallions), chopped
- 20g (¾oz) Thai basil, leaves picked
- 2 large eggs
- 2 pinches of crushed black pepper
- 2 tsp chilli oil

Heat a frying pan (skillet) without oil over a medium heat. Add the lạp xưởng sausage slices and toss for 30–40 seconds until they turn a bright, translucent red (or, if using chorizo, toss for 1–2 minutes until browned). Remove from the pan and set aside.

To the same pan, add the vegetable oil and sauté the garlic and lemongrass for 1 minute. Add the cooked noodles, soy sauce, fish sauce, sesame oil and sugar and cook, stirring, for 2–3 minutes, until the noodles are soft. Stir in the spring onions and most of the Thai basil, reserving a few leaves for the garnish, cooking for a further 2 minutes until everything is heated through. Then, remove from the heat and divide the noodles between your serving plates.

In the same pan, fry the eggs sunny-side up until the whites are set but the yolks remain runny. Place the eggs on top of the noodles and add the sliced sausage.

Sprinkle with the reserved Thai basil and the crushed black pepper, then drizzle over a little chilli oil to give your meal a delicious kick.

Serving Suggestion

The beauty of this dish is in its flexibility. You can swap the Vietnamese sausage for chorizo, scramble the eggs instead of frying them and use any noodles you prefer. Pre-cooked noodles work just as well too, so this is an easy meal to customize to your taste.

BÚN GÀ NƯỚNG SẢ

LEMONGRASS CHICKEN NOODLE BOWL

TAKES 30 MINUTES, PLUS MARINATING — SERVES 4

A street food classic, bún thịt nướng translates as 'grilled meat noodle' – a beautiful combination of words, especially when I'm hungry or catch a glimpse of sunshine in the garden. Known for its vibrant contrasts of flavour and texture, this dish brings together fragrant lemongrass-marinated grilled chicken, soft rice noodles and crisp herbs. You'll find me cooking it for our little family of three, or for a crowd of hundreds. It's a guaranteed crowd-pleaser and absolutely delicious!

1kg (2lb 4oz) boneless, skinless chicken thighs
400ml (14fl oz/1¾ cups) all-purpose marinade (see page 181)
4 lemongrass stalks, chopped
200g (7oz) vermicelli rice noodles, cooked according to the packet instructions
1 cucumber, julienned
200g (7oz) lamb's lettuce or mixed leaves
20g (¾oz) mint, leaves picked
20g (¾oz) Thai basil, leaves picked
20g (¾oz) coriander (cilantro), leaves picked
200g (7oz) daikon and carrot pickle (see page 180)

TO GARNISH AND SERVE
50g (1¾oz) salted roasted peanuts, crushed
4 tbsp crispy fried shallots (see page 180 for homemade)
4 tbsp ginger and chive oil (see page 179)
4 tsp chilli and lemongrass oil (see page 179)
400ml (14fl oz/1¾oz) nước chấm (see page 175)

In a baking tray, combine the chicken, all-purpose marinade and lemongrass. Cover and leave it to marinate for at least 30 minutes, or overnight in the fridge for a richer flavour (removing from the fridge 30 minutes before cooking to bring to room temperature).

Preheat the oven to 180°C/160°C fan/350°F/Gas 4. Place the chicken in the oven and cook for 25 minutes, or until cooked through and slightly charred. Remove from the oven and leave to rest for a few minutes before slicing it into thin strips.

Divide the cooked rice noodles between 4 serving bowls. Top with sliced grilled chicken, cucumber, salad leaves, herb leaves and pickles.

Garnish with the peanuts and crispy fried shallots, then drizzle over the ginger and chive oil, and the chilli and lemongrass oil to finish. Serve with the nước chấm on the side.

MÌ UDON CARBONARA

UDON CARBONARA

TAKES 20 MINUTES — SERVES 2

This take on the Italian classic carbonara introduces a Vietnamese twist by replacing spaghetti with chewy udon noodles and adding a few extra ingredients to bring bold, Asian flavours to the dish. The result is a delightful fusion of two culinary traditions, offering a fresh take on a beloved favourite.

100g (3½oz) pancetta (or guanciale), diced
1 garlic clove, finely chopped
1 shallot, finely chopped
1 red chilli, finely chopped
1 lemongrass stalk, finely chopped
4 large egg yolks
50g (1¾oz) pecorino cheese, finely grated
200g (7oz) udon noodles, cooked according to the packet instructions
2 pinches of coarsely ground black pepper
5g (⅙oz) Thai basil, leaves picked (optional)

In a large dry pan, sauté the pancetta over a medium heat for 2–3 minutes until crispy and it has released its oil. Add the garlic, shallot, chilli and lemongrass, then cook for a further minute.

In a small bowl, whisk 2 of the egg yolks and the pecorino together until smooth.

Remove the pan from the heat and immediately add the cooked udon noodles, tossing to coat them with the pancetta mix.

Slowly pour the egg yolk and cheese mixture over the noodles, stirring quickly to prevent the eggs from scrambling. Add a little water if needed to create a silky textured sauce.

Season with the black pepper, then top each serving with an egg yolk. A few Thai basil leaves to garnish add an extra layer of flavour and make a wonderful addition to this dish's profile.

Serving Suggestion

For an extra layer of flavour, sprinkle a little more pecorino on top. Pair with a crisp green side salad to bring a fresh balance to the meal.

CANH ĐẬU HŨ NON NẤU CÀ CHUA & THƠM

SILKEN TOFU, TOMATO AND PINEAPPLE SOUP

TAKES 35 MINUTES — SERVES 2

This recipe brings together silky tofu, the tangy sweetness of ripe tomatoes and the natural sourness of pineapple to create a vibrant yet balanced broth. Light, fragrant and gentle enough for all ages to enjoy.

1 tbsp vegetable oil
1 echalion shallot, chopped
3 garlic cloves, chopped
500ml (17fl oz/generous 2 cups) vegetable stock (broth)
2 tbsp umami paste
1 tbsp light soy sauce
1 tbsp brown sugar
20 cherry tomatoes
1 small pineapple, peeled, cored and cut into bite-sized chunks
300g (10½oz) silken tofu, cut into large cubes

TO FINISH
2 spring onions (scallions), chopped
1 red chilli, sliced
5g (⅙oz) coriander (cilantro), chopped
2 tbsp chilli and lemongrass oil (see page 179)
1 tsp coarsely ground black pepper

In a pot, heat the vegetable oil over a medium heat. Add the shallot and garlic and sauté until lightly browned.

Pour in the stock, then stir in the umami paste, soy sauce and sugar. Bring to the boil then add the cherry tomatoes and pineapple. Simmer over a medium heat for 10 minutes.

Gently add the tofu and cook for a further 5 minutes, without stirring too much, to avoid breaking it up.

Finish with the spring onions, sliced chilli, coriander, chilli and lemongrass oil and a sprinkle of black pepper.

CANH TÔM BÍ NGÒI

COURGETTE AND PRAWN SOUP

TAKES 20 MINUTES — SERVES 4

A light, refreshing traditional soup often found on family dinner tables to complement a more heavy meat dish. Traditionally made with winter melon, this version uses courgettes for a more accessible take, while still capturing the clean, delicate flavours of the original. I like that it's very different to what we see as a soup in the West – give it a try, you might love it as much as I do!

2 tbsp vegetable oil
2 garlic cloves, finely chopped
1 echalion shallot, finely chopped
200g (7oz) raw peeled king prawns (jumbo shrimp), roughly chopped
500ml (17fl oz/generous 2 cups) chicken stock (broth)
400g (14oz) courgettes (zucchini), julienned
½ tsp salt
1 tbsp fish sauce
1 tsp sugar

TO GARNISH
5 sprigs of coriander (cilantro), stalks and leaves chopped
2 spring onions (scallions), finely chopped
½ tsp coarsely ground black pepper

In a large pot, heat the vegetable oil over a medium heat. Add the garlic and shallot and sauté for 1–2 minutes, until fragrant and lightly golden.

Add the prawns and cook for 1 minute, stirring to break them into small pieces. Pour in the stock and bring to the boil, then add the courgettes and skim off any impurities.

Season with the salt, fish sauce and sugar. Simmer for 2 minutes until the courgettes are just tender but still slightly crisp.

Ladle into bowls and garnish with the coriander, spring onions and a sprinkle of black pepper.

Serving Suggestion
Serve this soup as part of a traditional Vietnamese-style meal with jasmine rice and a richer main dish. Its light, clean profile balances heartier flavours beautifully.

Make it Veggie
Swap the chicken stock for vegetable stock, fish sauce for light soy sauce, and simply leave out the prawns.

Soups and Noodles

MEAT

GÀ RÔ TI

ROTISSERIE SPATCHCOCK CHICKEN

TAKES 50 MINUTES, PLUS MARINATING — SERVES 4

Gà rô ti, a Vietnamese take on rotisserie chicken, gets its name from the French word 'rôti', meaning roasted. This recipe is even better when spatchcocked, helping the chicken cook evenly with beautifully crisp, caramelized skin. Marinated in a rich blend of flavours, the chicken is slow-cooked to perfection. Any leftovers are ideal for salads, sandwiches or noodle toppings, making it as versatile as it is simple to prepare.

1 whole chicken, spatchcocked (see Note)
200ml (7fl oz) all-purpose marinade (see page 181)
1 tbsp ground turmeric
1 tbsp paprika
1 tbsp five-spice powder
30g (1oz) butter

Place the spatchcocked chicken in a large bowl and coat thoroughly with the all-purpose marinade, turmeric, paprika and five-spice. Make sure every bit of the chicken is evenly coated.

Cover and refrigerate for at least 30 minutes, or ideally overnight, to let the flavours really sink in (removing from the fridge 30 minutes before cooking to bring to room temperature).

Preheat the oven to 180°C/160°C fan/350°F/Gas 4. Rub a baking tray with the butter.

Place the chicken skin-side up on the prepared tray. Roast for 40 minutes, then increase the heat to 200°C/180°C fan/400°F/Gas 6 and roast for a final 5 minutes to crisp up the skin.

Serving Suggestion

For an authentic Vietnamese meal, serve with a crusty French baguette and rice noodles, or pair with hot, fluffy jasmine rice for the perfect balance of spice and comfort.

Note

To spatchcock a chicken, place it breast-side down on a chopping board. Using sturdy scissors or poultry shears, cut along each side of the backbone to remove it (save it for making stock). Flip the chicken over so it is breast-side up and press down firmly on the breastbone with the heel of your hand, to flatten it out.

CỪU HẦM GIA VỊ VÀ NƯỚC CỐT DỪA

SPICED LAMB SHANK STEW

TAKES 3¼ HOURS — SERVES 2

This lamb shank stew brings together tender, slow-cooked lamb with rich, fragrant spices. Combining the heartiness of a stew with the warming aromatics of a traditional Vietnamese curry, it's the perfect dish to enjoy on chilly days or when you're in the mood for something comforting and full of flavour.

2 tbsp vegetable oil
2 lamb shanks, 800g–1kg (1lb 12oz–2lb 4oz) in total
8 shallots, finely chopped
3 garlic cloves, finely chopped
50g (1¾oz) ginger, peeled and finely chopped
2 lemongrass stalks, bruised and tied into a knot
1 tsp five-spice powder
1 tsp ground turmeric
1 tsp chilli powder
1 tsp paprika
3 red chillies, left whole
400ml (14fl oz) coconut cream
500ml (17fl oz/generous 2 cups) beef bone broth
1 tbsp fish sauce
1 tbsp brown sugar

TO GARNISH AND SERVE
4 sprigs of Thai basil
4 sprigs of coriander (cilantro)
4 stems of fresh curry leaves, finely julienned
10g (⅓oz) unsalted roasted peanuts, crushed
½ lime, cut into wedges

Preheat the oven to 160°C/140°C fan/320°F/Gas 2½.

In a large flameproof casserole, heat the vegetable oil over a medium-high heat. When hot, sear the lamb shanks for 8–10 minutes, until all sides are browned. Remove from the pan and set aside.

Lower the heat to medium. Add the shallots, garlic, ginger and lemongrass, then sauté for 2–3 minutes until browned.

Stir in the five-spice, turmeric, chilli powder, paprika and chillies, then cook for 2 minutes to release the aromas of the spices.

Return the lamb shanks to the pan. Pour in the coconut cream and beef bone broth, and stir together well. Then stir in the fish sauce and sugar.

Cover the pot with a lid, transfer to the oven and bake for 2½–3 hours, or until the lamb shanks are tender and the meat is falling off the bone.

Carefully remove the lamb shanks and ladle the stew into your serving bowls. Place the lamb on top, garnishing with the fresh Thai basil, coriander and curry leaves, finally sprinkling over the crushed peanuts to finish. Serve with a squeeze of lime juice.

Serving Suggestion
This oven-baked lamb shank stew is perfect with crusty French bread, echoing the traditional way bò kho (beef stew) is enjoyed in Vietnam. Alternatively, serve it over steamed jasmine rice or rice noodles to soak up that rich and flavoursome broth.

THỊT BÊ HẦM SẢ

OSSO BUCO LEMONGRASS STEW

TAKES: 2½ HOURS — SERVES 2

Inspired by the classic Vietnamese bò kho (beef stew), this one offers a comforting twist on a traditional favourite. Tender, slow-cooked veal, infused with fresh lemongrass and warm spices, makes for a deliciously rich and hearty dish that's warming on every bite. With its robust flavours and bold aromatics, it's perfect for family gatherings or any special occasion. This stew is bound to become a firm family favourite.

550–650g (1lb 2oz–1lb 7oz) osso buco (2 pieces on the bone)
4 pinches of salt
2 tsp sesame oil
2 tbsp vegetable oil
100g (3½oz) baby carrots
100g (3½oz) baby parsnips, halved
8 garlic cloves, peeled
4 shallots, thickly sliced
50g (1¾oz) ginger, sliced and crushed
4 lemongrass stalks, crushed
2 litres (4¼ pints) coconut water
100g (3½oz) oyster mushrooms
1 tbsp cornflour (cornstarch), dissolved in 3 tbsp water

FOR THE SEASONING
10 star anise
20g (¾oz) cinnamon stick
1 tsp ground coriander
200g (7oz) tomato purée (paste)
1 tsp salt
2 tbsp sugar
4 tbsp fish sauce
4 tbsp sesame oil
2 tsp paprika
2 beef stock (bouillon) cubes, crumbled
1 tbsp chilli powder (adjust to taste)

TO GARNISH
2 red chillies, left whole
2 spring onions (scallions), halved
1 tsp coarsely ground black pepper

Preheat the oven to 165°C/145°C fan/330°F/Gas 2½.

Season the osso buco with the salt and sesame oil, making sure you cover both sides evenly, and set aside.

Heat a large flameproof casserole over a high heat and add the vegetable oil. Once hot, in separate batches, add the carrots, parsnips, garlic, shallots, ginger and lemongrass, and sear until charred. Remove everything to a plate or bowl as they are seared. Avoid overcrowding the pan and don't add extra oil unless really needed, as this will achieve better charring.

Add the osso buco and sear until charred, then place the seared garlic, lemongrass and ginger back in the pan and add all the seasoning ingredients and coconut water. Cover with a lid, place in the oven and cook for 1¾ hours. Add the seared carrots and parsnips and return to the oven for 30 minutes.

Remove from the oven and place on the stovetop. Stir in the mushrooms and cornflour mixture, then cook over a medium-high heat for 5 minutes, until it thickens slightly.

Garnish with the chillies, spring onions and black pepper, and serve piping hot.

Serving Suggestion

This stew is best enjoyed with a crispy baguette. Spread with cream cheese for an extra touch of richness! Alternatively, it can be enjoyed with steamed jasmine rice or noodles to soak up all that delicious broth.

SƯỜN NƯỚNG

STICKY PORK RIBS

TAKES 45 MINUTES, PLUS MARINATING — SERVES 2

Vietnamese pork ribs are a popular choice at family gatherings and street food stalls alike, known for their smoky, caramelized exterior and tender meat. Whether served at a casual lunch or for a lively dinner, these ribs bring together simple yet bold flavours that make them a go-to choice for all occasions.

500g (1lb 2oz) baby pork ribs
200ml (7fl oz) all-purpose marinade (see page 181)
3 tbsp honey
1 tbsp paprika

TO SERVE
3 tbsp ginger and chive oil (see page 179)
2 tbsp chilli and lemongrass oil (see page 179)

Place the ribs, bone-side up, on a board and use a knife to lift and peel away the thin, shiny membrane. Removing this layer allows the marinade to penetrate more deeply and prevents a chewy texture when eating.

Line a baking tray with baking parchment. Add the ribs, all-purpose marinade, honey and paprika, then rub everything over and into the ribs. Marinate for at least 30 minutes, or overnight in the fridge for a deeper flavour (removing from the fridge 30 minutes before cooking to bring to room temperature).

Preheat the oven to 200°C/180°C fan/400°F/Gas 6. Bake the ribs for 25–30 minutes, flipping them over halfway through.

Serve piping hot, drizzled with ginger and chive oil and chilli and lemongrass oil for the ultimate Vietnamese sticky ribs.

Serving Suggestion

This recipe pairs perfectly with steamed jasmine rice, allowing the rich flavours of the ribs to stand out. A side of pickled vegetables adds a sharp contrast, balancing the sweetness of the caramelized glaze, while a crisp cucumber and fresh herb salad provide a refreshing finish.

THỊT KHO TRỨNG CÚT & MĂNG

BRAISED PORK, QUAIL'S EGGS AND BAMBOO SHOOTS

TAKES 2 HOURS — SERVES 4

Some meals do more than fill you up. They conjure memories of family, tradition and comfort. This is most definitely one of those dishes; it reminds me of the simple joy of gathering round the dinner table, surrounded by family, with the aroma of the dish simmering away and filling the air.

Growing up, this rich, meaty dish was reserved for special occasions, like Tết (Lunar New Year). It was everybody's favourite, yet for me it was bittersweet as it made me miss my grandparents, who weren't with us in London. All the while filling my soul with warmth from the memories evoked. As well as making my belly happy, of course.

Thịt kho trứng is more than just a dish to me. It's a connection to home, a memory of shared moments and a bowlful of love.

- 8 tbsp golden caster (superfine) sugar
- 2 tbsp water
- 1kg (2lb 4oz) belly pork, cut into 3cm (1¼ inch) cubes
- 1 litre (34fl oz/generous 4 cups) coconut water
- 80ml (3fl oz) fish sauce
- 8 garlic cloves, peeled
- 8 star anise
- 6 shallots, halved lengthways
- 250g (9oz) drained, canned bamboo shoots
- 12 quail's eggs, hard-boiled for 4 minutes, then peeled
- 5 red bird's eye chillies, left whole

Preheat the oven to 160°C/140°C fan/320°F/Gas 2½.

Add the sugar to a flameproof casserole and place over a medium heat. Let it melt and bubble slowly, without stirring (keep a close eye on it). Once it turns amber, add the water and let it deepen to a rich dark brown.

Add the pork belly and cook for 5–6 minutes, allowing the meat to sear and catch a little colour.

Pour in the coconut water, followed by the fish sauce, garlic, star anise and shallots.

Cover, transfer to the oven and cook for 1½ hours. Add the bamboo shoots, quail's eggs and chillies, increase the oven temperature to 180°C/160°C fan/350°F/Gas 4 and cook for a further 20 minutes.

Transfer the dish back to the stovetop. Remove the garlic, star anise, and shallots. Cook, uncovered, over a high heat for 10 minutes to caramelize and thicken the sauce.

Serve hot with jasmine rice, pickles, or a fresh salad, and savour one of Vietnam's most comforting classics.

CÀ RI GÀ

LEMONGRASS AND COCONUT CHICKEN CURRY

TAKES 45 MINUTES — SERVES 4

Vietnamese chicken curry is a comforting, aromatic dish with a rich, creamy sauce. Blending French colonial influence with traditional Vietnamese flavours, this dish features tender chicken simmered in coconut milk with a fragrant mix of spices. It's utterly addictive – an instant family favourite! Traditionally served with rice or a crusty French baguette, it perfectly showcases the fusion of Vietnamese and French culinary traditions

1kg (2lb 4oz) bone-in, skin-on chicken thighs
½ tbsp salt
3 tbsp ground turmeric
2 tbsp vegetable oil
250g (9oz) baby potatoes, halved

FOR THE CURRY SAUCE
800ml (1¾ pints) coconut cream (at least 70% coconut)
3 echalion shallots, chopped
4 garlic cloves, chopped
80g (3oz) ginger, peeled and chopped
1 tbsp curry powder
1 tbsp paprika
1 tbsp chilli powder
4 tbsp fish sauce
2 tbsp brown sugar
2 chicken stock (bouillon) cubes, crumbled
8–10 fresh lime leaves
4 lemongrass stalks, halved and crushed

TO GARNISH
4 tsp crispy fried shallots (see page 180 for homemade)
4 pinches of coarsely ground black pepper
Thai basil and coriander (cilantro)

Rub the chicken thighs with the salt and turmeric, making sure the skin is well coated.

Heat the vegetable oil in a large sauté pan over a high heat. Add the potatoes and the chicken, skin-side down. Sear for 7–8 minutes until the chicken skin is crisp and the potatoes are slightly browned.

Flip the chicken skin-side up. Pour in the coconut cream, avoiding the chicken skin to keep it crispy. Add the remaining curry sauce ingredients. Reduce the heat to a gentle simmer and cook for 25 minutes, or until the chicken is tender and cooked through. Taste and adjust the balance of flavours if needed, adding more fish sauce or sugar if you like.

Garnish with the crispy fried shallots, black pepper and some Thai basil and coriander.

Serving Suggestion

Cà ri gà is best enjoyed with a portion of fluffy jasmine rice or a crusty French baguette, both of which are perfect for soaking up the delicious curry sauce.

CÁNH GÀ CHIÊN NƯỚC MẮM

GARLIC FISH SAUCE CHICKEN WINGS

TAKES 35 MINUTES — SERVES 4

A go-to in many Vietnamese households, these wings are a staple at family meals – and no party is complete without them. With crispy golden skin and that moreish savoury-sweet flavour, it's easy to see why.

4 tbsp fish sauce
2 tbsp honey
2 tbsp garlic powder
4 chicken stock (bouillon) cubes, crumbled
1 tbsp coarsely ground black pepper
4 tbsp cornflour (cornstarch)
1kg (2lb 4oz) chicken wings, cut into wingettes and drumettes
Vegetable oil, for shallow-frying

TO SERVE
Crispy fried garlic (shop-bought)
Sliced red chillies (optional)
1 lime, cut into wedges
2 tbsp fish sauce (optional)

In a large bowl, mix the fish sauce, honey, garlic powder, stock cubes, black pepper and cornflour together until smooth. Add the chicken wings and use your hands to massage the rub in well, coating each piece thoroughly.

Add a 2cm (¾ inch) depth of vegetable oil to a large sauté pan and heat to 175°C (345°F). To check if the oil is ready, dip a wooden chopstick into it; if bubbles form around the chopstick, it's ready.

Fry the chicken wings in batches, ensuring you don't overcrowd the pan, for 8–10 minutes, or until golden brown and crispy. Remove and drain on a plate lined with paper towel.

Serve the wings hot, topped with crispy fried garlic and sliced chilli if you like, with lime wedges on the side. For the brave, try dipping them in fish sauce.

Serving Suggestion
Turn these crispy wings into a balanced meal with jasmine rice and a mixed leaf salad. I love using UK-grown greens like rocket (arugula) and watercress, paired with sliced cucumber, radishes and cherry tomatoes, tossed in a simple French dressing.

GÀ KHO GỪNG

GINGER CARAMELIZED CHICKEN

TAKES 25 MINUTES — SERVES 4

Vietnamese comfort food at its best, gà kho gừng is a dish that brings together a perfect balance of spices for a cosy, satisfying meal. It's the kind of dish that reminds me of noisy family dinners, with steam rising from the rice cooker and the chicken simmering away on the stove, filling the house with a fragrant aroma. Gà kho gừng is more than just a dish; it's a slice of home, a taste of tradition and a bowlful of love. This simplified version brings that comfort to your table in under 30 minutes.

650g (1lb 7oz) skinless, boneless chicken thighs
1 tsp salt
1 tsp coarsely ground black pepper
2 tbsp vegetable oil

FOR THE SAUCE
4 tbsp golden caster (superfine) sugar
100ml (3½fl oz) coconut water
3 tbsp fish sauce
6 garlic cloves, finely chopped
100g (3½oz) ginger, peeled and julienned
1 spring onion (scallion), thinly sliced
1 red chilli, thinly sliced

In a bowl, season the chicken thighs with the salt and black pepper, rubbing it in evenly.

Heat the vegetable oil in a sauté pan over a high heat. Sear the chicken for 3 minutes on each side until nicely charred. Remove and set aside.

Wipe the pan clean, then add the sugar over a medium heat. Cook until it turns a rich caramel colour, watching carefully to avoid burning.

Immediately return the chicken to the pan, coating it in the caramel. Add the coconut water, fish sauce and garlic. Simmer over a medium-low heat for 10–12 minutes, until the sauce becomes sticky and caramelized.

Add the ginger, spring onion and red chilli, stir through for 1 minute, then take off the heat and serve.

Serving Suggestion
Serve family-style with jasmine rice and a side of stir-fried vegetables, pickles or a fresh cucumber salad.

HEO NƯỚNG MẬT ONG HONEY

GRILLED PORK RICE

TAKES 30 MINUTES, PLUS (OPTIONAL) OVERNIGHT MARINATING — SERVES 4

This is the dish I picture tucking into at a tiny family-run café on a buzzing street in Ho Chi Minh City. It arrives fast, the meat hot and perfectly charred from a live fire grill. The plate's always heaped with rice and fresh salads, but trust me, go for double meat. It's like doubling up your patty on your favourite burger. Yes, you might need a nap after, but you'll be smiling. And the best bit? You can make this at home.

500g (1lb 2oz) pork neck steak
4 tomatoes, quartered

FOR THE MARINADE
200ml (7fl oz) all-purpose marinade (see page 181)
2 tbsp honey
2 lemongrass stalks, chopped

TO SERVE
4 portions of cooked rice
4 eggs, fried sunny-side up
1 lettuce, leaves torn
1 cucumber, sliced
5g (⅛oz) mint, leaves picked
5g (⅛oz) dill, leaves picked
40g (1½oz) daikon and carrot pickle (see page 180)
200ml (7fl oz) nước chấm (see page 175)
4 tsp ginger and chive oil (see page 179)
4 tsp crispy fried shallots (see page 180 for homemade)

In a small bowl, mix the marinade ingredients together. In a bowl, coat the pork with the marinade. Ideally, leave it to marinate overnight in the fridge for best flavour, or at least 30 minutes (removing from the fridge 30 minutes before cooking to bring to room temperature).

Preheat the oven to 180°C/160°C fan/350°F/Gas 4.

Place the pork on a baking tray and roast for 15 minutes. Add the tomatoes to the tray and cook for another 10 minutes, until both are charred and caramelized.

Serve with rice, a fried egg, lettuce, cucumber, herbs, pickles and 'all the trimmings': nước chấm, ginger and chive oil and crispy fried shallots.

VỊT VỚI CAM, ĐÀO VÀ SẢ

CLEMENTINE, PEAR AND PEACH LEMONGRASS DUCK

TAKES 25 MINUTES — SERVES 2

This is a delightful fusion of juicy, tender duck with a fruity, savoury sauce that's guaranteed to impress. The vibrant mix of sweet oranges, peaches and pears complements the rich duck and aromatic lemongrass beautifully. It's an easy yet elegant dish, perfect for a special dinner or a cosy meal at home.

2 duck breasts, about 350–400g (10–14oz) each
2 pinches of salt
2 tsp vegetable oil
2 lemongrass stalks, crushed
1 peach, halved and stoned
2 pears (any firm variety), cored and quartered
4 baby courgettes (zucchini), sliced diagonally into bite-sized pieces
6 shallots, halved lengthways
4 garlic cloves, peeled
Juice of 4 clementines, strained
2 tbsp light soy sauce
2 tbsp sesame oil
1 tbsp honey (or 1 tbsp sugar)
2 tbsp ginger and chive oil (see page 179), to finish

Score the skin of the duck breasts lightly and season both sides with half the salt.

Place the duck breasts skin-side down in a cold pan. Place the pan over a medium heat and sear the duck until the skin turns golden and crispy, about 5–6 minutes. Flip the duck breasts and sear the other side for an additional 8–10 minutes for medium, or longer if you prefer it more well done. Remove from the pan and leave to rest for 5 minutes before slicing thinly.

Using the same pan, increase the heat to high and add the vegetable oil. When hot, add the lemongrass, peach halves, pears, courgettes, shallots and garlic cloves, charring them for 4–5 minutes, until they are browned and slightly caramelized. Remove everything except the lemongrass and garlic from the pan.

Add the clementine juice, soy sauce, sesame oil, honey and the remaining salt. Stir and simmer the sauce for a few minutes until it thickens slightly.

Return the peaches, pears and courgettes to the pan and cook for 2–3 minutes until slightly softened but still al dente.

To serve, spread the sauce, fruit and vegetables on a plate and arrange the sliced duck breast on top. Finish with the ginger and chive oil.

SƯỜN BÒ CAY

RED-HOT SHORT RIBS

TAKES 2 HOURS (OR 45-50 MINUTES IN THE OVEN) — SERVES 4

Exactly as the name suggests, this dish is not for the faint-hearted. But trust me, the heat is worth it. This is my show-off recipe, a guaranteed crowd-pleaser. Slow-braised beef short ribs that melt in your mouth, drenched in a rich, fragrant sauce of chilli, paprika, tomato and lemongrass.

1 tbsp vegetable oil
8 garlic cloves, peeled
8 star anise
4 beef short ribs, about 250–300g (9–10½oz) each, evenly salted
2 clusters of cherry tomatoes on the vine (about 250g/9oz in total)

FOR THE HOT SAUCE
2 tbsp chilli powder
2 tbsp paprika
4 tbsp tomato purée (paste)
4 lemongrass stalks, crushed
500ml (17fl oz/generous 2 cups) beef stock (broth)
2 beef stock (bouillon) cubes, crumbled
1 tbsp fish sauce
2 tbsp sesame oil
1 tsp ground turmeric

TO GARNISH
2 red chillies, sliced
5g (⅙oz) coriander (cilantro), leaves picked
1 spring onion (scallion), finely sliced on the diagonal

Blitz all of the hot sauce ingredients together in a food processor, then set aside.

Heat a flameproof casserole over a medium-high heat, add the vegetable oil, then sauté the garlic and star anise. Add the ribs and sear on all sides for 1–2 minutes until browned.

Cover with a lid and simmer over a low heat for 2 hours, adding the tomatoes for the final 10 minutes. (Alternatively, bake in the oven at 180°C/160°C fan/350°F/Gas 4 for 45-50 minutes.)

Garnish with the chilli, coriander and spring onion.

Serving Suggestion
For an authentic Vietnamese meal, serve with a crusty French baguette and rice noodles, or pair with hot, fluffy jasmine rice for the perfect balance of spice and comfort.

THỊT HEO QUAY & NƯỚC MẮM TÁO

Roast Pork and Nước Chấm Apple Salsa

TAKES 3 HOURS, PLUS 3 DAYS DRY-BRINING — SERVES 4

Roast pork is a celebratory dish in Vietnamese culture, loved for its crispy skin and tender, flavourful meat. Traditionally served for festivities like New Year and weddings, the golden crackling is said to bring good fortune and the rich meat, fertility and success. This recipe is simple but requires patience – trust me, it's worth the wait!

500g (1lb 2oz) belly pork (see tips for perfect crackling, overleaf)
1 tbsp white vinegar
6 tbsp salt

FOR THE APPLE SALSA
2 green apples, peeled, cored and finely diced
200ml (7fl oz) nước chấm (see page 175)
80ml (2¾fl oz) olive oil
5g (⅛oz) coriander (cilantro), stalks and leaves roughly chopped
5g (⅛oz) mint leaves, roughly chopped

FOR THE SOY GLAZE
2 tbsp sesame oil
3 tbsp light soy sauce
3 tbsp honey
2 tbsp balsamic vinegar
1 tsp coarsely ground black pepper

Add 5cm (2 inches) of water to a pan and bring to the boil. Add the pork, skin-side down, ensuring the water only covers the skin, not the meat. Cook over a medium heat for 20 minutes. Flip the meat and cook for 1 minute. Remove from the heat and leave to cool for 10 minutes.

Remove the pork from the pan. Pat dry thoroughly, then score the skin in a criss-cross pattern with a sharp knife, taking care not to cut into the meat. Rub the vinegar all over the skin, then cover the surface with a thick layer of salt. Refrigerate, uncovered, for 3 days to dry out the skin.

Preheat the oven to 200°C/180°C fan/400°F/Gas 6. Remove the salt and place the pork on a wire rack over an oven tray. Roast for 10 minutes, then reduce the oven temperature to 150°C/130°C fan/300°F/Gas 2 and cook for a further 2¼ hours.

Increase the oven temperature to 200°C/180°C fan/400°F/Gas 6 and cook for a final 4–5 minutes for really crispy skin. Leave to rest for 5 minutes, then slice.

In a bowl, mix all the apple salsa together. In a separate bowl, combine the soy glaze ingredients, along with any roasting juices from the oven tray. To serve, drizzle the glaze over the sliced pork. Serve the apple salsa on the side or spooned straight over the top, for extra flavour.

Serving Suggestion

For a fuller meal, enjoy with a baguette 'bánh mì style', or go the traditional Vietnamese route by serving it with vermicelli rice noodles, pickles, fresh herbs and nước chấm. However you decide to serve this pork, happy diners are guaranteed!

SECRET (NOT SO SECRET) TIPS FOR PERFECT CRACKLING:

Our elders often pass down time-honoured techniques, some requiring patience, others involving skills mastered over time. Over the years, I've taken these hard-earned tips and refined them into a method that anyone can follow with ease. These simple steps will ensure your crackling turns out perfect every time!

Dry the Skin Thoroughly
Drying the skin eliminates surface moisture, which helps avoid steam occurring during cooking (as steam softens the skin). Leaving it uncovered in the fridge helps the moisture evaporate, ensuring the fat underneath can render properly, which is key to achieving crisp skin.

Score the Skin Properly
Scoring increases the surface area and allows heat to penetrate evenly, helping the fat render and preventing the skin from shrinking unevenly. It also helps the fat escape, enhancing the crisping process.

Apply Vinegar
The acetic acid in vinegar breaks down proteins in the skin, promoting crisping during roasting. This helps the skin brown evenly and gives it that perfect crackling texture.

Use a Dry Rub
Salt draws out moisture from the skin, keeping it dry and improving the chance of crisping.

Roast on a High Heat
High heat evaporates moisture quickly and renders the fat beneath the skin, leading to a perfectly blistered and crispy finish. Starting at a high temperature ensures crisp skin while preventing the meat from drying out.

Increase the Temperature Towards the End
A final blast of high heat evaporates any remaining moisture and finishes off the fat rendering, enhancing the crispness without overcooking the meat. This results in a crunchy surface and succulent meat underneath.

Use a Rack
Elevating the meat on a rack lets hot air circulate around it, ensuring an even crisping. This prevents the skin from becoming soggy and helps the fat render evenly.

Rest Before Slicing
Letting the meat rest allows the juices to settle, keeping the meat moist and stopping it from softening the crackling. This ensures both the crispness of the crackling and the tenderness of the meat.

VỊT NƯỚNG NGŨ VỊ HƯƠNG

SPICED ROAST DUCK

TAKES 2 HOURS, PLUS 1–3 DAYS' DRY-BRINING — SERVES 4

Nose-to-tail cooking is something I was brought up with, and am pleased to see it becoming second nature to more and more people. A great example of this is the duck, because so much of it can be used: the meat, skin, bones, fat and even offal are all used in Vietnamese cooking. This roast duck is a personal favourite, never failing to impress when I cook for friends and family. It's beautifully infused with rich aromatics, meaning that the meat shines as the star of your salad, the highlight of your noodle dish or as another roast dinner option. Yes, it takes time and patience, but every minute is worth it, I promise.

Don't let the duck carcass or any leftover meat go to waste: check out page 70 for a delicious way to turn it into a brand-new dish!

1 whole duck, about 1.5kg (3lb 5oz)
4 tbsp salt
1 tbsp light soy sauce
1 tbsp honey
100ml (3½fl oz) ginger and chive oil (see page 179), to serve

FOR THE STUFFING
1 lemongrass stalk, halved and crushed
1 red chilli, halved
5g (⅛oz) ginger, sliced and crushed
4 garlic cloves, crushed (unpeeled)
6 star anise
1 cinnamon stick

Place the duck on a metal rack over a large tray. Pour boiling water over the duck to tighten the skin and remove any excess fat. Drain thoroughly, then pat dry and rub generously with the salt. Place, uncovered, in the fridge to dry-brine for 24 hours, or up to 3 days for a perfect flavour (removing from the fridge 30 minutes before roasting to bring to room temperature).

Preheat the oven to 180°C/160°C fan/350°F/Gas 4.

Remove the salt, then stuff the duck cavity with the lemongrass, chilli, ginger, garlic, star anise and cinnamon, then secure the opening with toothpicks.

Roast in the oven for 1¾ hours. Remove the toothpicks and use one to prick the skin, all over the duck. Rub the skin with a light layer of soy sauce and a very thin layer of honey.

Increase the oven temperature to 200°C/180°C fan/400°F/Gas 6 and roast for a further 40 minutes, or until the skin is golden and crispy. Remove from the oven and leave to rest for at least 10 minutes before carving.

Carve, and serve drizzled with the ginger and chive oil.

FISH AND SEAFOOD

CÁ KHO TỘ

CLAY POT HAKE

TAKES 20 MINUTES — SERVES 1

This traditional Vietnamese dish of fish braised in a clay pot originates from the Mekong Delta, where catfish is plentiful. In this version, I use hake – a mild, flaky white fish that works beautifully with the rich, caramelized sauce. It's an incredibly humble dish, yet full of deep, satisfying flavours, all of which pair perfectly with a steaming hot bowl of jasmine rice.

1 tbsp vegetable oil
2 shallots, finely chopped
3 garlic cloves, finely chopped
200g (7oz) hake fillet, skinned
200ml (7fl oz) coconut water
2 tbsp fish sauce
2 tbsp golden caster (superfine) sugar
1 red chilli, left whole
10g (⅓oz) green peppercorns
1 tsp coarsely ground black pepper

Heat the vegetable oil in a clay pot (or a regular pan if you don't have one) over a medium heat. Add the shallots and garlic and sauté until light brown, then place the fish in the pot. Add the coconut water, fish sauce and sugar and cook, uncovered, for 8 minutes, then turn the fish over and add the chilli and green peppercorns. Cook for a further 10 minutes.

Once the fish is tender and the sauce has reduced to a sticky consistency, remove from the heat. Garnish with coarse black pepper and you're ready to tuck in.

Serving Suggestion

Cá kho tộ is a robust and flavoursome dish that should be enjoyed as the centrepiece of a meal. It pairs wonderfully with steamed jasmine rice, which helps to balance the rich, savoury sauce. For a more complete Vietnamese meal, consider adding a vegetable stir-fry or side. Cavolo nero and roasted garlic stir fry (see page 151) or a soup like butternut squash and coconut soup (see page 78) will work beautifully.

CHẢ CÁ TUYẾT VÀ KHOAI TÂY

COD AND CHIVE POTATO FISH CAKES

TAKES 45 MINUTES — SERVES 4

These fish cakes take inspiration from classic Vietnamese flavours often paired with seafood. Made with cod, mashed potatoes, dill and chives, they're pan-fried until golden and crisp on the outside, with a soft, fluffy centre. My twist is a mustard-infused nước chấm, which adds a wonderfully tangy kick to the traditional dipping sauce. While it might not be what traditionalists expect, it's a flavour combination that works beautifully.

- 3 medium floury potatoes, peeled and diced
- 3 tbsp vegetable oil
- 400g (14oz) cod fillets, skinned and pin-boned
- 30g (1oz) dill, chopped, plus extra fronds, left whole, to garnish
- 2 tbsp chopped chives
- Zest and juice of 1 lemon
- 1 tsp salt
- 2 tsp coarsely ground black pepper
- 1 egg, beaten
- 100g (3½oz) breadcrumbs

FOR THE MUSTARD NƯỚC CHẤM
- 400ml (14fl oz/1¾ cups) nước chấm (see page 175)
- 1 tbsp wholegrain mustard
- 10g (⅓oz) dill, chopped

TO GARNISH AND SERVE
- 4 sprigs of mint, leaves picked
- 1 lemon, cut into wedges

Place the diced potatoes in a deep sauté pan, cover with water and bring to the boil, then cook for 10–15 minutes until tender. Drain and mash, then transfer to a bowl and set aside. Wipe the pan clean.

While the potatoes are boiling, mix the mustard nước chấm ingredients together in a bowl, stirring until well combined, then set aside.

Return the pan to a medium heat, adding 1 tablespoon of oil. Place in the cod fillets and cook for 3–4 minutes on each side, until the fish is cooked through and flakes easily with a fork. Remove the cod from the pan, flake into small pieces and add to the mashed potatoes.

Add the dill, chives, lemon zest and juice, salt and pepper, then mix until well combined. Divide the mixture evenly into 4 and shape into patties. Dip each patty in the beaten egg, then coat with breadcrumbs.

In the same pan, heat the remaining oil over a medium heat. Add the fish cakes and shallow-fry for 3–4 minutes on each side, until golden brown and crispy.

Plate the fish cakes, then drizzle over a generous serving of the mustard nước chấm, garnish with mint leaves and dill fronds and serve with a lemon wedge.

Serving Suggestion
For a light, flavour-packed lunch, serve with daikon and carrot pickle (see page 180) and salad leaves.

CÁ NGỪ VỚI KIWI VÀ QUÝT

KIWI AND CLEMENTINE TUNA CEVICHE

TAKES 30 MINUTES — SERVES 4

This recipe offers a fresh take on the classic Vietnamese lime-cured salad by swapping out beef for delicate yellowfin tuna. The zesty lime marinade lifts the tuna, while the kiwi and clementine add a sweet, tangy contrast that complements the fish sauce and fresh herbs. The mix of juicy fruit, tender fish and crunchy peanuts makes this salad a refreshing choice for a light meal or appetizer, especially on warm days.

This salad makes an excellent starter for a refined dinner party, or it can be served as a light main course for a more intimate gathering. Its balance of textures and flavours will easily elevate any occasion, making it a standout dish.

300g (10½oz) yellowfin tuna, thinly sliced
1 red onion, thinly sliced
1 kiwi, peeled and thinly sliced
2 clementines, segmented and removed from membranes, skin reserved and thinly sliced
1 lime, finely sliced
5g (⅙oz) mint leaves
5g (⅙oz) coriander (cilantro) leaves
1 tbsp salted peanuts, lightly crushed
1 tbsp crispy fried shallots (see page 180 for homemade)

FOR THE DRESSING
200ml (7fl oz) nước chấm (see page 180)
Juice of 2 clementines

In a small bowl, combine the dressing ingredients.

On a serving plate, arrange the tuna and pour over enough dressing to completely cover it. Leave to cure for at least 20 minutes, but no longer than 30 minutes to avoid pickling the fish.

To serve, top the cured tuna with the red onion, kiwi, clementine segments, clementine peel, lime slices, mint and coriander. Drizzle with the remaining dressing, then finish with a sprinkle of peanuts and the crispy fried shallots for a refreshingly gorgeous dish!

Serving Suggestion

This elegant and delicate dish is best enjoyed immediately to appreciate the fresh flavours of the tuna and fruit. Pair it with a crisp white wine, or a light, citrusy beer to enhance the vibrant notes of the lime and complement the subtle richness of the tuna.

NGHÊU HẤP NƯỚC CỐT DỪA

MUSSELS IN COCONUT CREAM

TAKES 20 MINUTES — SERVES 2

This recipe brings together the rich creaminess of coconut milk and the natural sweetness of fresh mussels. The sauce is simple yet versatile, great for any seafood or even just vegetables. It's one of those 'no-sauce-left-behind' dishes that'll quickly become a favourite in your kitchen. The perfect excuse to bring out your favourite wine!

1 tbsp vegetable oil
2 lemongrass stalks, cut into 5cm (2 inch) pieces and crushed
4 shallots, thinly sliced
3 garlic cloves, finely chopped
200ml (7fl oz) coconut cream
1 chicken stock (bouillon) cube, crumbled
1 tbsp fish sauce
1 tsp sugar
1kg (2lb 4oz) mussels, cleaned and debearded
5g (⅙oz) coriander (cilantro), stalks and leaves chopped
5g (⅙oz) Thai basil, leaves chopped
1 red chilli, thinly sliced
1 lime, cut into wedges

TO SERVE
1 baguette
30g (1oz) butter

Heat the vegetable oil in a large, deep pan over a medium heat. Add the crushed lemongrass to the pan and cook for 1 minute until fragrant. Add the shallots and garlic, sautéing for 2 minutes until they become a golden brown colour.

Tip in the coconut cream, stock cube, fish sauce and sugar, stirring to combine, then bring the mixture to a gentle simmer.

Add the mussels to the pan, covering them with the coconut cream sauce. Cover the pan with a lid and cook for 5–7 minutes, or until the mussels have opened. Discard any mussels that do not open.

Stir in the coriander, Thai basil and chilli slices just before serving, reserving a few of each to garnish when plating.

Finally, squeeze a little fresh lime juice over just before serving, with buttered baguette to soak up the creamy coconut sauce.

Serving Suggestion
A side of lightly dressed mixed greens adds the perfect balance, making for a well-rounded and satisfying meal.

CÁ NƯỚNG SẢ & SỐT BƠ

SEA BREAM WITH LEMONGRASS AND HERB BUTTER

TAKES 40 MINUTES — SERVES 2-3

An ever-popular celebratory dish in Vietnam, cá nướng sả is known for its aromatic flavours and natural simplicity. Traditionally made with catfish, here I opt for the more accessible sea bream, adding a touch of butter for extra richness. The whole fish is stuffed with a fragrant mix of lemongrass, ginger and fish sauce. In Vietnam, it's typically grilled over live fire for that irresistible char. At home, I suggest oven baking for an easier method that doesn't compromise on flavour – just be sure to cook the fish whole, so the bones release their natural swetness and infuse beautifully with the lemongrass. The result is perfectly balanced seasoning and tender, succulent meat.

1 whole sea bream (about 250–300g/9–10½oz), descaled
2 lemongrass stalks, crushed
1 lemon, sliced into thin rounds

FOR THE HERB BUTTER

3g (⅛oz) ginger, peeled and roughly chopped
4 garlic cloves, peeled
3 tsp fish sauce
30g (1oz) butter, plus extra for greasing
2 tsp brown sugar
2 tbsp sesame oil
10g (⅓oz) coriander (cilantro), leaves and stems

TO GARNISH AND SERVE

3 spring onions (scallions), thinly julienned and soaked in cold water
1 red chilli, thinly sliced on the diagonal
Sprinkling of crushed unsalted roasted peanuts

Preheat the oven to 200°C/180°C fan/400°F/Gas 6.

Blitz all the herb butter ingredients together (reserving a few coriander leaves for the garnish) in a food processor. Set aside.

Score 3 or 4 diagonal cuts on both sides of the sea bream. Fill the cuts with the herb butter. Then open up the belly of the fish and fill it with more of the herb butter, the crushed lemongrass and the lemon slices.

Place the stuffed sea bream on a greased baking tray and cook in the oven for 25 minutes, until the flesh is opaque and flakes easily with a fork.

Plate the bream, drizzling the butter sauce from the tray over the top. Garnish with the spring onions, reserved coriander leaves and chilli. Finally, sprinkle the roasted peanuts over the top for that satisfying crunch on the bite.

Serving Suggestion

The beauty of this dish is its versatility. In Vietnam, the most popular way it's eaten is as a sharing meal, with plenty of fresh herbs, rice paper rolls, and a dipping sauce, like nước chấm (see page 175). It's often accompanied by jasmine rice for those who prefer a more filling meal. Alternatively, carving out the fillet and serving it with roasted vegetables is also a delicious option.

CÁ NƯỚNG BƠ

BAKED DOVER SOLE AND FISH SAUCE BUTTER

TAKES 25 MINUTES — SERVES 2

This recipe brings together citrus, spice and a rich butter sauce, all while showcasing the depth of fish sauce and the delicate flavour of Dover sole. Infused with the fresh aromas of dill and Thai basil, this dish is inspired by Vietnam's vibrant coastal cooking, where seafood is the natural star. Cooking the fish whole and on the bone enhances its flavour and keeps the texture silky. Perfect for a special meal, this recipe offers a true taste of the sea with a fragrant Vietnamese twist.

1 whole Dover sole (or 2 Dover sole fillets)
2 pinches of salt
2 pinches of coarsely ground black pepper
1 lemon, thinly sliced into rings
3 tbsp unsalted butter, melted
1 tbsp fish sauce
1 tsp sugar
1 red chilli, finely chopped
2 garlic cloves, finely chopped
2 shallots, thinly sliced

TO GARNISH
1 tbsp chopped dill
1 tbsp chopped Thai basil

Preheat the oven to 190°C/170°C fan/375°F/Gas 5. Line a baking tray with baking parchment or lightly grease it with butter.

Place the Dover sole on the baking tray, seasoning both sides with the salt and pepper. Lay the lemon rings evenly on top of the fish.

In a small bowl, combine the melted butter, fish sauce, sugar, chilli, garlic and shallots, stirring until the sugar dissolves and the mixture is well combined.

Pour the butter sauce over the fish (whole or fillets), ensuring it is well coated. Bake in the preheated oven for 15–18 minutes (10–15 minutes for fillets), or until the fish is cooked through and flakes easily with a fork.

To garnish, sprinkle the chopped dill and Thai basil over the fish before serving.

Serving Suggestion

Serve with a side of steamed jasmine rice to soak up the delicious butter sauce, along with more fresh herbs (more of the same or different), and cucumber for added freshness. Also, adding a side of stir-fried greens like water spinach or Tenderstem broccoli will bring balance to the meal.

Fish and Seafood

CÁ CHIÊN SỐT CÀ

PAN-FRIED COD IN TOMATO SALSA

TAKES 30 MINUTES — SERVES 2

Traditionally, this dish features a whole fried fish served with a tomato-based sauce that's rich in umami and has a touch of sweetness. My take uses cod fillets for a quicker and more accessible version, with additional flavours like Romano peppers and oyster mushrooms, adding layers of depth for a dish that's both familiar and novel. It's the perfect way to enjoy the flavours of Vietnam in a simple, weeknight-friendly meal.

2 cod fillets
2 pinches of salt
5 tsp vegetable oil
100g (3½oz) oyster mushrooms, roughly chopped

FOR THE TOMATO SALSA
1 tbsp vegetable oil
1 Romano pepper, deseeded and finely chopped
2 shallots, diced
3 garlic cloves, finely chopped
3 ripe tomatoes, deseeded and diced
5g (⅙oz) coriander (cilantro), leaves picked, stalks finely chopped
1 tsp fish sauce
1 tsp light soy sauce
2 tsp sugar
Pinch of salt
1 tbsp sesame oil

TO FINISH AND GARNISH
1 tbsp ginger and chive oil (see page 179)
1 tbsp crispy fried shallots (see page 180)
2 sprigs of dill

Lightly salt both sides of the cod fillets and set aside.

In a frying pan (skillet), heat 1 teaspoon of the vegetable oil over a high heat. Lightly char the mushrooms for about 30 seconds, then remove and set aside.

To the same pan, add the 1 tablespoon of vegetable oil for the sauce and reduce the heat to medium. Add the Romano pepper, shallots and garlic. Sauté for 2 minutes until fragrant. Add the tomatoes and coriander. Cook for another 2 minutes until the tomatoes begin to soften. Stir in the fish sauce, soy sauce, sugar and salt. Sauté for a further 2 minutes until the sauce thickens slightly. Drizzle in the sesame oil, mix well, then transfer the salsa to a bowl and set aside. Return the pan to the heat.

Add the remaining vegetable oil to the pan and place in the cod fillets. Cook over a low-medium heat for 6 minutes with a lid on, allowing the fish to steam slightly. Flip the fillets to cook the other side for an additional 4–5 minutes until cooked through.

To serve, spread the warm tomato salsa on the base of a serving dish. Arrange the sautéed mushrooms on top, then place the fish fillets over the mushrooms. Finish with ginger and chive oil and crispy fried shallots, garnish with the dill, and serve immediately.

Serving Suggestion

This dish pairs perfectly with a fresh salad. My preference is a simple mix of lettuce, rocket (arugula), cucumber, mint, coriander and Thai basil. For a full meal, serve with steamed jasmine rice and a vegetable stir-fry for a little crunch. A light, clear broth can be added for a refreshing, traditional touch.

SALADS AND VEGETABLES

CHÂN VỊT HẦM VỚI GỎI DƯA HẤU

CONFIT DUCK WATERMELON SALAD

TAKES 3½ HOURS, PLUS CURING — SERVES 2

This dish combines the richness of duck confit, infused with bold Vietnamese flavours, and the vibrant freshness of a watermelon salad. The sweet, tangy tamarind dressing ties everything together, creating a perfect balance of flavours. Definitely one to bookmark for watermelon season!

2 duck legs
1 tbsp flaky sea salt
2 garlic cloves, crushed
2 tsp five-spice powder
500ml (17fl oz/generous 2 cups) duck fat (or enough to submerge the duck legs)
8 star anise
10g (⅓oz) cinnamon stick

FOR THE SALAD
200g (7oz) watermelon, cubed
100g (3½oz) lamb's lettuce
10g (⅓oz) Thai basil, leaves picked
10g (⅓oz) coriander (cilantro), leaves picked
300ml (10fl oz/1¼ cups) tamarind sauce (see page 175)

Rub the duck legs with the salt, garlic and five-spice, then leave to cure in the fridge for at least 1 hour, or overnight if possible.

Rinse the duck legs, then pat dry. Preheat the oven to 120°C/100°C fan/250°F/Gas ½.

In a deep ovenproof dish, submerge the duck legs in duck fat, adding the star anise and cinnamon stick. Cook in the oven for 2½ hours, until the meat is fall-off-the-bone tender. Remove from the oven and leave to cool in the fat.

Increase the oven temperature to 180°C/160°C fan/350°F/Gas 4.

Pour the fat out of the dish, then place back in the oven and roast the duck legs for a further 25–30 minutes until the skin is crispy and golden.

While the duck is roasting, prepare the salad by gently tossing together the watermelon, lamb's lettuce, Thai basil and coriander in a large bowl.

Drizzle the tamarind sauce over the watermelon salad, tossing lightly to ensure an even coating.

Either plate the crispy confit duck and serve with the salad or pull the meat from the bones, slice or tear into pieces and use to top the salad.

GÀ LÚC LẮC GỎI QUẢ MƠ

SHAKING CHICKEN AND APRICOT SALAD

TAKES 20 MINUTES, PLUS MARINATING — SERVES 2

I love experimenting with recipes to make them my own, and here is a great example. This Vietnamese comfort food showcases how small tweaks can make a huge difference to a dish. Shaking beef is a classic Vietnamese recipe celebrated for its vibrant flavours, but I often prefer a lighter twist with this chicken version.

Tender, marinated fillet paired with fresh, juicy apricot slices on a bed of mixed greens creates a delightful combination. Perfect for a quick yet impressive meal, this dish brings a taste of Vietnam into your kitchen with minimal fuss and maximum flavour.

2 boneless, skinless chicken breasts, cut into 2cm (¾ inch) cubes
150ml (5fl oz) all-purpose marinade (see page 181)
2 tsp vegetable oil
2 tsp chilli and lemongrass oil (see page 179)
60g (2oz) lamb's lettuce
3 apricots, stoned and sliced into bite-sized wedges
12 cherry tomatoes, halved
1 red onion, thinly sliced
80ml (3fl oz) nước chấm (see page 175)

In a bowl, combine the chicken with the all-purpose marinade. Mix well then leave to marinate for at least 30 minutes, or overnight in the fridge for a deeper flavour (removing from the fridge 30 minutes before cooking to bring to room temperature).

Heat a frying pan (skillet) over a high heat and add the vegetable oil. When hot, add the chicken and sear for 1 minute to char the edges and lock in flavour. Turn the heat down to medium and cook for 10–12 minutes until cooked through. Finish with the chilli and lemongrass oil.

While the chicken is cooking, toss the lamb's lettuce, apricots, tomatoes and red onion with nước chấm on a large serving plate. Top with the hot chicken and serve immediately.

Serving Suggestion

For a complete Vietnamese-style meal, enjoy this with a bowl of fragrant jasmine rice and a cold beer. That said, it's just as lovely on its own!

GỎI CUA VÀ SU HÀO

CRAB, KOHLRABI AND DILL MUSTARD SALAD

TAKES 20 MINUTES — SERVES 2

This light and refreshing salad combines the delicate sweetness of crab with the crisp crunch of kohlrabi. While not a traditional Vietnamese salad, it draws on the country's love for fresh seafood and refreshing flavours. The zesty mustard-infused dressing adds a Western twist, making it a unique yet familiar addition to any Vietnamese-inspired meal.

100g (3½oz) white crab meat
1 medium kohlrabi, peeled and julienned
Pinch each of salt and coarsely ground black pepper
2 chicory (endive) bulbs, 1 red and 1 white, leaves sliced diagonally
250g (9oz) fennel, thinly shaved

FOR THE DRESSING
2 tbsp mayonnaise
2 tsp wholegrain mustard
1 tsp English mustard
4 tbsp olive oil
1 tsp lemon juice
1 tsp fish sauce
4 garlic cloves, finely chopped
1 red chilli, finely chopped
5g (⅛oz) mint, finely chopped
10g (⅓oz) dill, finely chopped
2 pinches of coarsely ground black pepper

In a small bowl, mix together the dressing ingredients, reserving some dill to garnish, until smooth and well combined.

In a large mixing bowl, combine the crab meat and kohlrabi, seasoning with the salt and pepper. Gently toss with the prepared dressing until evenly coated.

To serve, toss the crab and kohlrabi salad with the chicory and fennel and garnish with the reserved dill.

Serving Suggestion

This is perfect as a light appetizer, refreshing side dish, or sophisticated canapé. It pairs beautifully with a glass of chilled champagne or a crisp white wine, making it an ideal choice for a refined start to any meal. It also works wonderfully alongside a cheese board or fried dishes such as chả giò spring rolls (see page 39), offering a fresh contrast to richer flavours.

GỎI BƯỞI TÔM

POMELO AND PRAWN PEA SHOOT SALAD

TAKES 20 MINUTES — SERVES 4

This is a light and refreshing Vietnamese salad, originating from the southern Mekong Delta, where pomelos are abundant. Traditionally, it combines the tangy sweetness of pomelo with fresh prawns and fragrant herbs, symbolizing prosperity in Vietnamese culture. This version adds avocado for a creamy texture, bringing a new layer of richness to the dish.

In a Western setting, pomelo can be swapped with grapefruit, and it would be just as delicious. Purple perilla (also known as shisho leaves) is available in most Asian stores. For a quicker option, ready-cooked prawns work well and save time without losing any flavour.

280g (10oz) cooked, peeled king prawns (jumbo shrimp)
1 large pomelo or grapefruit, segments removed from their thin membranes and cut into bite-sized pieces
1 avocado, flesh cut into small chunks
1 green (unripe) mango, peeled and julienned
80g (3oz) pea shoots
5g (⅙oz) purple perilla (see recipe introduction), leaves picked
5g (⅙oz) Thai basil, leaves picked
5g (⅙oz) mint, leaves picked
400ml (14fl oz/1¾ cups) tamarind sauce (see page 175)
10g (⅓oz) crispy fried shallots (see page 180 for homemade)

In a large bowl, combine the prawns, pomelo, avocado and mango, along with the pea shoots, perilla, Thai basil and mint.

Drizzle the tamarind sauce over the salad ingredients, tossing gently to ensure everything is evenly coated.

Plate up the salad for serving, then sprinkle over the crispy fried shallots.

Serving Suggestion

Traditionally, this salad is served as a starter, often accompanied by rice crackers, bánh phồng tôm, for an extra crunch. This salad also makes a great side dish to complement many of the recipes in this book, helping create a well-rounded, balanced meal.

Make it Veggie

Simply omit the prawns, and use sweet soy sauce (see page 178) for the dressing.

GỎI BÒ SỐT CHUA NGỌT

SWEET AND SOUR BEEF SALAD

TAKES 30 MINUTES, PLUS MARINATING — SERVES 4

Gỏi bò sốt chua ngọt is a vibrant, refreshing Vietnamese beef salad which draws influence from Thai cuisine. It's made with tender slices of beef, crunchy vegetables and fresh herbs, all tossed in a tangy dressing that adds a lovely zing. In Vietnam, salads like this are a staple at family meals, offering a light, zesty contrast to richer dishes. Not only is this salad delicious, it's also incredibly versatile, perfect for a quick lunch, starter or light dinner. It's an excellent introduction to the five key flavours that capture the essence of Vietnamese cuisine while using ingredients readily available in the West.

400–500g (14oz–1lb 2oz) rib-eye beef steak
100ml (3½fl oz) all-purpose marinade (see page 181)
1 green (unripe) mango, peeled
1 cucumber
1 green apple, cored
1 red onion
100g (3½oz) mangetout (sugar snap peas)
100g (3½oz) mixed colour cherry tomatoes
5g (⅙oz) coriander (cilantro), leaves picked
5g (⅙oz) mint, leaves picked
5g (⅙oz) Thai basil, leaves picked
1 tbsp vegetable oil

FOR THE DRESSING
200ml (7fl oz) tamarind sauce (see page 175)
Juice of 1 orange
2 tbsp sriracha sauce
2 lemongrass stalks, finely chopped

TO GARNISH AND SERVE
2 tbsp unsalted roasted peanuts, crushed
1 pack of ready-made prawn crackers

Place the steak in a bowl, coat in the all-purpose marinade and set aside to marinate, for up to 3 hours in the fridge if you have time, to let the meat fully absorb the flavours (removing from the fridge 30 minutes before cooking to bring to room temperature).

Julienne the mango and cucumber, then thinly slice the apple, red onion and mangetout. Halve the cherry tomatoes. Place it all in a large mixing bowl along with the herbs. Add the dressing ingredients and toss everything together until evenly coated. Set aside.

Heat the vegetable oil in a large frying pan (skillet) over a high heat. Sear the steak for about 1½ minutes on each side for rare, or longer according to your preference. Remove from the pan and let rest for 5 minutes, before slicing into strips and adding to the salad.

Transfer the salad to a large serving platter or divide between individual plates. Garnish with crushed peanuts for extra crunch, and serve with prawn crackers on the side, perfect for scooping up every bite.

Serving Suggestion

Simple, fresh sides are the perfect complement to this zesty beef salad, balancing its bold flavours. As noted, dishes like this are often enjoyed as part of everyday family meals in Vietnam, providing a lighter counterpoint to richer mains. It's typically paired with steamed jasmine rice, which serves as a neutral base, letting the salad's complex flavours shine. It's perfect as part of a shared meal, but it also works beautifully as a stand-alone salad if you're keeping it light.

CÁ CHIÊN GIÒN SỐT ME HÀNH ĐỎ

CRISPY TAMARIND AND RED ONION FRIED FISH

TAKES 20 MINUTES — SERVES 2

Some dishes need to be eaten piping hot, but for this traditional dish it's all about the contrasts between hot and cold, and crunchy and soft. Hot, flaky fish meets crisp vegetables, creating a balance that makes every mouthful stand out. Vietnamese cooking is all about harmony, from fresh and bold to delicate and crisp, and this is a perfect example. Light yet packed with flavour, it has been a firm favourite in my kitchen since I was little, and remains so to this day!

2 sea bass fillets, skin on
2 tbsp cornflour (cornstarch)
100ml (3½fl oz) vegetable oil
Lemon wedges, to serve

FOR THE SALAD
1 fennel bulb, thinly shaved
5g (⅛oz) dill, leaves picked
5g (⅛oz) coriander (cilantro), leaves picked, stalks finely chopped
5g (⅛oz) chives, chopped into 1cm (½ inch) pieces
1 red onion, finely sliced
1 lime, zest pared and finely julienned
2 lemongrass stalks, finely chopped
5g (⅛oz) fresh lime leaves, finely julienned
400ml (14fl oz/1¾ cups) tamarind sauce (see page 175)

In a large mixing bowl, combine all the salad ingredients, tossing lightly in the tamarind sauce to coat.

Coat the fish fillets in cornflour, then heat the oil in a frying pan (skillet), add the fish, skin-side down, and shallow-fry for 2–3 minutes on each side, until golden and crispy.

Plate the salad, then break the fish into large chunks and place on top. Serve with lemon wedges on the side for squeezing over. Enjoy on its own or, like me, with a bowl of jasmine rice or vermicelli rice noodles.

GỎI GÀ CHIÊN BƠ

CRISPY BUTTER CHICKEN SALAD

TAKES 45 MINUTES — SERVES 2

This salad is traditionally served with Vietnamese chicken porridge, cháo gà, a comforting family favourite often enjoyed when feeling under the weather. Nutritious and soul-warming, it's the Vietnamese equivalent of a mother's hug. It also pairs beautifully with most braised or grilled dishes. Why not remove the chicken and swap it in for coleslaw at your next barbecue? With its tangy dressing and fresh herbs, it makes an ideal side for many dishes in this book or a satisfying stand-alone meal.

4 boneless, skin-on chicken thighs, patted dry
4 pinches of salt
30g (1oz) butter
½ white cabbage, thinly sliced
1 carrot, julienned
½ cucumber, deseeded and julienned
1 red onion, thinly sliced
5g (⅙oz) coriander (cilantro), finely chopped
5g (⅙oz) Vietnamese mint (or regular mint), leaves picked
2 tbsp ginger and chive oil (see page 179)
250ml (9fl oz/1 cup) nước chấm (see page 175)
2 tbsp unsalted roasted peanuts, roughly crushed, to garnish

Lightly salt the chicken thighs, then place them skin-side down in a cold frying pan (skillet). Turn the heat to medium and cook for 15–20 minutes, until the skin is golden and crispy. Flip the chicken over, add the butter and cook for an additional 5–10 minutes until fully cooked through.

In a large bowl, mix the cabbage, carrot, cucumber and red onion, along with the coriander and mint. Pour in the ginger and chive oil and nước chấm, and toss to combine.

Slice the cooked chicken into strips. Plate the salad ready for serving and place the chicken on top.

To garnish, sprinkle the roasted peanuts over the salad for a lovely added crunch to finish.

Serving Suggestion

This salad is traditionally served with Vietnamese chicken porridge, but it pairs beautifully with most braised or grilled dishes. Its tangy dressing and fresh vegetables balance out the rich flavours of more substantial meals, making it an ideal side for many of the dishes in this book or as a stand-alone dish.

CÀ RỐT NƯỚNG MẬT ONG VỚI SỐT BƠ

HONEY-ROASTED CARROTS IN BƠ SAUCE

TAKES 30 MINUTES — SERVES 4

Delightfully simple yet packed with flavour, this recipe pairs sweet honey-roasted carrots with a luscious Vietnamese bơ sauce traditionally used on the classic street food dish, bánh mì. The creamy sauce, inspired by the French classic known as beurre blanc, is enhanced with umami notes from fish sauce and the warmth of garlic. Topped with fresh herbs and crunchy peanuts, it's a dish that balances sweetness, creaminess and savoury depth beautifully.

500g (1lb 2oz) heritage carrots, peeled and halved
1 tbsp honey
2 tbsp olive oil
2 pinches of flaky sea salt
1 tbsp finely chopped coriander (cilantro) stalks and leaves
1 tbsp finely chopped dill
5g (⅛oz) unsalted roasted peanuts, roughly chopped

FOR THE BƠ SAUCE
8 egg yolks
1 tsp fish sauce
1 tsp coarsely ground black pepper
150ml (5fl oz) roasted garlic oil (see page 178 for homemade)
5 shallots, ideally red, finely chopped

Preheat the oven to 200°C/180°C fan/400°F/Gas 6.

In a roasting tray, toss the carrots with the honey, olive oil and salt. Roast for 12–15 minutes, until tender with a slight crunch still.

While the carrots are roasting, prepare the bơ sauce. In a small bowl, whisk together the egg yolks, fish sauce and black pepper. Once the mixture lightens in colour, slowly drizzle in the garlic oil while continuing to whisk. Keep whisking for 5–8 minutes until the sauce thickens to a smooth, mayo-like consistency. Stir in the shallots.

Spread a generous layer of the bơ sauce on a serving plate, then arrange the honey-roasted carrots on top.

Garnish with the coriander and dill, then sprinkle over the peanuts for a delicious crunch to finish.

Serving Suggestion
Serve these carrots as a vibrant side dish alongside grilled fish or meat dishes for a complete meal.

BẮP CẢI NƯỚNG SỐT TƯƠNG NGỌT

CHARRED CABBAGE WITH 'SỐT TƯƠNG NGỌT' PEANUT SAUCE

TAKES 30 MINUTES — SERVES 4

This recipe brings out the smoky, nutty and spicy notes associated with sốt tương ngọt, the peanut sauce synonymous with summer rolls. It's so versatile and flavourful that you'll want to dip just about everything in it!

2 tbsp vegetable oil
1 Savoy cabbage, cut into 8 wedges
1 tbsp fried shallots, to garnish
2 tsp sunflower and pumpkin seeds (or 2 tsp mixed seeds)
2 tsp chilli oil, for drizzling

FOR THE PEANUT SAUCE
2 tbsp hoisin sauce
1 tbsp peanut butter
2 tsp sriracha sauce
2 garlic cloves, finely chopped
½ lime, juiced, or 1 tbsp lime juice
120ml (4fl oz) boiling water

Heat a large pan over a high heat and add the vegetable oil. Place the cabbage wedges in the pan, then let them char for about 5 minutes per side until they develop a nice, deep colour. You may need to do this in batches.

While the cabbage is cooking, combine all the peanut sauce ingredients, except the boiling water, in a small bowl. Gradually pour in the boiling water, continuously stirring until the sauce is smooth and creamy.

Arrange the charred cabbage wedges on a serving plate. Drizzle the peanut sauce evenly over the wedges, then garnish with the fried shallots, sprinkle over the mixed seeds and finish with a drizzle of chilli oil to taste.

Serving Suggestion

This charred cabbage is a versatile dish that pairs beautifully with grilled meats or vegetables, or as part of a larger meal. Serve alongside steamed jasmine rice or as a unique side to a barbecue (grill). The smoky, nutty peanut sauce adds a lovely depth of flavour, making it a great option for a light lunch or an impressive side dish for a shared meal with friends and family.

Salads and Vegetables

CẢI XÀO DẦU TỎI NƯỚNG

CAVOLO NERO AND ROASTED GARLIC STIR-FRY

TAKES 5 MINUTES — SERVES 2

This dish draws inspiration from Vietnam's love for stir-frying fresh greens such as morning glory and Asian lettuce. The quick stir-fry method keeps the leaves green, crisp and full of flavour, which is essential to get right. A glug of my roasted garlic oil adds a lovely depth, blending traditional Vietnamese techniques with some Western touches.

2 tbsp light soy sauce
½ tsp sugar
1 tsp lime juice
5 roasted garlic cloves and 3 tbsp roasted garlic oil (see page 170)
1 tbsp vegetable oil
200g (7oz) cavolo nero, torn into bite-sized pieces (stems removed)
Pinch of coarsely ground black pepper
Dried garlic flakes (shop bought), to garnish

In a small bowl, mix the soy sauce, sugar, lime juice and roasted garlic cloves. Use a spoon to lightly break the garlic into chunks, without mashing it, then stir in the roasted garlic oil.

Heat the vegetable oil in a pan over a high heat. Add the cavolo nero and toss for 45 seconds to 1 minute, ensuring it is hot but remains green and crunchy. Then remove from the heat and transfer to a plate.

Drizzle the sauce over the cavolo nero, sprinkle over the black pepper and garlic flakes to finish, and serve immediately.

Serving Suggestion

Traditionally, stir-fried greens in Vietnam are served alongside rice and other family-style dishes. You could pair this dish with grilled chicken, salmon or tofu for a healthy, balanced meal. It's also delicious with a side of quinoa or roasted potatoes for added texture and substance.

Salads and Vegetables

CHẠO TÔM CÀ NƯỚNG

PRAWN-STUFFED BAKED HEIRLOOM TOMATOES

TAKES 30 MINUTES — SERVES 4

Inspired by the classic Vietnamese prawn cake dish, flame-grilled on sugarcane sticks, this recipe offers a modern twist that's both elegant and bursting with flavour. The bouncy, seasoned prawn mixture is paired with ripe heirloom tomatoes, giving a juicy, sweet contrast with every bite. This recipe is really versatile, working beautifully with peppers, aubergine or portobello mushrooms; perfect as a simple starter or easily turned into a main course with the addition of rice or noodles. It's a quick, delicious and visually stunning option for any occasion. Plus, it can be prepped the night before, making it a fantastic choice for dinner parties.

4 large heirloom tomatoes
10g (¼oz) butter

FOR THE PRAWN CAKE
250g (9oz) raw king prawns (jumbo shrimp), peeled and deveined
½ tsp garlic powder
1 chicken stock (bouillon) cube, crumbled
1 tsp coarsely ground black pepper
1 tsp sugar
3 tsp sesame oil
1 tsp fish sauce

FOR THE GLAZE
50ml (3½ tbsp) light soy sauce
100ml (3½fl oz) vegetable oil
1 tsp sugar
Juice of ½ lime
2 tsp chilli oil
2 spring onions (scallions), finely chopped

Preheat the oven to 200°C/180°C fan/400°F/Gas 6.

Slice off 1–2cm (½–¾ inch) from the top of each tomato. Using a metal teaspoon, carefully remove the seeds, leaving a hollow centre. Set the prepared tomatoes aside.

In a blender or food processor, combine all the prawn cake ingredients and blitz for 8–10 seconds, ensuring the mixture retains some chunky texture.

Grease a baking tray with the butter to prevent sticking. Generously fill each hollowed tomato with the prawn mixture. Place the stuffed tomatoes on the tray and bake for 15–20 minutes, or until the edges turn golden.

While the tomatoes are baking, combine all the glaze ingredients in a small pan. Bring the mixture to the boil over a low heat, stirring gently. Once the sugar dissolves and the sauce thickens slightly, with bubbles forming on the surface, remove from the heat.

Plate the baked tomatoes and drizzle them with the soy onion glaze, or serve the glaze on the side as a dip.

Serving Suggestion
Enjoy this dish as a vibrant starter or a light main course with the addition of jasmine rice and a simple vegetable side.

NẤM SÒ ÁP SỐT BƠ NGHỆ

OYSTER MUSHROOMS SAUTÉED IN TURMERIC BUTTER

TAKES 20 MINUTES — SERVES 2

I adore mushrooms of every kind and would happily put them on just about anything. It's not just the flavour I love, but also that spongy texture, perfect for soaking up all the sauces. When I cook mushrooms, I try not to do too much to them; a good char is often all they need to bring out their natural flavour. Sometimes, the beauty of food lies in its simplicity, reminding us that less truly is more.

200g (7oz) oyster mushrooms
2 slices of sourdough bread, toasted
2 tsp garlic mayo
2 tsp crispy fried shallots (see page 180 for homemade)

FOR THE TURMERIC BUTTER
60g (2¼oz) butter
1 tbsp fish sauce
2 tsp honey
2 garlic cloves, finely sliced
1 tsp ground turmeric
10g (⅓oz) thyme, leaves picked

Heat a frying pan (skillet) over a medium heat and add all the sauce ingredients. Stir gently until the butter melts and combines with the honey to form a smooth sauce.

Add the oyster mushrooms, spacing them out evenly in the pan to ensure they fry rather than steam. Cook on both sides for 3–4 minutes until brown. Avoid overcrowding the pan.

Spread the toast with the garlic mayo, pile the mushrooms on to the toast and sprinkle with crispy fried shallots.

Serving Suggestion
This dish makes a lovely light lunch, perfect for when you're feeling peckish and want something quick. For a heartier meal, serve the mushrooms with a fresh green salad or as a side to steak or a roast dinner.

CÀ TÍM THỊT HEO TIÊU

SHIITAKE MUSHROOMS AND CURRY LEAF AUBERGINES

TAKES 20 MINUTES — SERVES 2

Whether you call it aubergine or eggplant, it's a versatile vegetable that holds a special place in Vietnamese cuisine. Growing up, I enjoyed it in many forms: grilled, steamed, braised, pickled, even raw in salads. Across Vietnam, aubergine is a staple ingredient, as it is often served as a vegetable side in family-style meals. Here, it takes centre stage, paired with savoury shiitake mushrooms and the aromatic pop of curry leaves.

2 tbsp vegetable oil
1 large aubergine (eggplant), sliced on the diagonal
50g (1¾oz) dried shiitake mushrooms, soaked, drained and cut into bite-sized pieces
30g (1oz) fresh curry leaves
3 tbsp vegan oyster sauce
1 tbsp light soy sauce
1 tsp sugar
2 tsp garlic powder
2 tsp coarsely ground black pepper

Heat 1 tablespoon of the vegetable oil in a frying pan (skillet) or griddle (grill) pan over a high heat. Sear the aubergine slices for 2–3 minutes on each side until nicely charred all over. Remove and arrange on a serving plate.

Wipe the pan clean and add the remaining oil. Add the mushrooms, curry leaves, mushroom oyster sauce, soy sauce, sugar and garlic powder, stirring together to ensure the mushrooms are well coated in the sauce. Cook for 3–4 minutes, until the mushrooms are tender and the curry leaves are crisping up.

Pour the mushroom mixture directly over the aubergine slices, sprinkle over the black pepper and serve immediately.

Serving Suggestion

This dish is best enjoyed with steamed jasmine rice to balance the rich umami flavours. It also makes a fantastic vegetable side alongside grilled meats or fish.

BÔNG CẢI TRẮNG NƯỚNG

BAKED CHIMICHURRI CAULIFLOWER

TAKES 30 MINUTES — SERVES 2

A flavour-packed dish that combines the earthy warmth of spiced roasted cauliflower with a zesty herb Vietnamese chimichurri. This effortless recipe is deliciously beautiful!

1 cauliflower, cut into bite-sized florets
1 tsp paprika
1 tsp salt
1 tsp ground turmeric
4 tbsp olive oil

FOR THE CHIMICHURRI
10g (⅓oz) parsley, leaves finely chopped
10g (⅓oz) coriander (cilantro), stalks and leaves finely chopped
10g (⅓oz) mint, leaves finely chopped
1 echalion shallot, finely chopped
200ml (7fl oz) nước chấm (see page 175)
2 tbsp chilli and lemongrass oil (see page 179)

Preheat the oven to 200°C/180°C fan/400°F/Gas 6.

On a baking tray, toss the cauliflower with the paprika, salt, turmeric and olive oil until evenly coated. Roast for 20 minutes, or until golden at the edges but still with a little bite.

Meanwhile, combine all the chimichurri ingredients in a bowl and mix well.

Once the cauliflower is cooked, transfer to a serving plate and drizzle generously with the chimichurri.

Make it Veggie
Switch the nước chấm for the sweet soy sauce on page 178.

Salads and Vegetables

KHOAI LANG & NẤM RỪNG NẤU NƯỚC CỐT DỪA

CREAMY SWEET POTATO AND WILD MUSHROOMS

TAKES 40 MINUTES — SERVES 4

In Vietnamese cooking, coconut is the go-to ingredient for creating a rich, smooth texture. In this dish its natural creaminess pairs beautifully with the umami of mushrooms and complements the sweetness of the potatoes. Comforting served over hot jasmine rice, or just as satisfying on its own.

1 tbsp vegetable oil

700g (1lb 9oz) sweet potatoes, peeled and cut into 3cm (1¼ inch) chunks

3 lemongrass stalks, halved and crushed

6 fresh lime leaves

1 tbsp golden caster (superfine) sugar

4 garlic cloves, chopped

800ml (1¾ pints/3½ cups) coconut cream

1 tbsp light soy sauce

2 tbsp umami paste

200g (7oz) wild mushrooms, cut into even sizes

TO GARNISH

5g (⅛oz) coriander (cilantro), leaves chopped

1 tbsp crispy fried shallots (see page 180 for homemade)

Preheat the oven to 200°C/180°C fan/400°F/Gas 6.

Heat the vegetable oil in a flameproof casserole over a high heat, add the sweet potato, lemongrass, lime leaves and sugar and sauté for 3–4 minutes until lightly browned. Stir in the garlic, then immediately add the coconut cream, soy sauce and umami paste. Cover with a lid, transfer to the oven and bake for 25 minutes.

Add the mushrooms, stir and return to the oven for a further 5 minutes.

Transfer to a serving dish and garnish with coriander and crispy fried shallots.

SWEETS

BÁNH CHEESECAKE VỊ CÀ PHÊ VÀ ĐẬU PHỘNG MẶN

SALTED PEANUT AND COFFEE CHEESECAKE

TAKES 30 MINUTES, PLUS CHILLING — SERVES 6

This is a no-bake cheesecake with a unique Viet twist on the classic recipe, adding the rich, bold flavours of Vietnamese coffee and contrasting it with the sweetness of condensed milk. It's a perfect treat for coffee lovers, combining iconic Eastern flavours in a light and creamy cheesecake.

150g (5oz) digestive biscuits (graham crackers), crushed
50g (1¾oz) salted peanuts, finely chopped
75g (3oz) unsalted butter, melted

FOR THE FILLING
600g (1lb 5oz) cream cheese, softened to room temperature
200ml (7fl oz) condensed milk
3 tbsp instant coffee powder (decaf for a family-friendly version)
1 tsp vanilla extract
200ml (7fl oz) double (heavy) cream, whipped to soft peaks
2 tsp gelatine powder, dissolved in 2 tbsp warm water

FOR THE TOPPING
1 tbsp ground coffee
1 tbsp condensed milk
30g (1oz) salted peanuts, roughly chopped

In a mixing bowl, combine the crushed biscuits, peanuts and melted butter, mixing until the crumbs are evenly coated.

Press the mixture into the base of an 18cm (7 inch) springform cake tin (pan), using the back of a spoon to create an even layer. Place in the fridge to chill while you prepare the filling.

In a large mixing bowl, whisk the cream cheese until soft and fluffy. Gradually add the condensed milk, continuing to whisk until fully mixed. Stir in the coffee powder and vanilla extract, mixing until the ingredients are well combined.

Gently fold in the whipped cream until the mixture is light and fluffy. Then add the dissolved gelatine and mix until thoroughly combined.

Pour the cheesecake filling over the chilled base, smoothing the top with a spatula.

Cover the tin with clingfilm (plastic wrap) and refrigerate for at least 4 hours, or until the cheesecake is fully set.

Before serving, dust the top of the cheesecake with the ground coffee, drizzle lightly with condensed milk, then sprinkle with the salted peanuts to finish.

Serving Suggestion
Serve with a cup of traditional Vietnamese iced coffee or tea for a perfect pairing of rich, creamy flavours.

BÁNH QUY SÔ-CÔ-LA ỚT

CHILLI CHOCOLATE COOKIES

TAKES 30 MINUTES — MAKES 12

This recipe is a must-try for anyone looking for a bold twist on a classic treat. It blends the aromatic flavours of Vietnamese cuisine into the moreish sweetness of a cookie. The fragrant lemongrass and hint of fresh chilli add a spicy kick that beautifully balances the rich white chocolate, making this cookie both unexpected and delicious.

100g (3½oz) salted butter, softened
150ml (5fl oz) condensed milk
1 large egg
½ tsp vanilla extract
1 tbsp finely chopped lemongrass
1 tbsp deseeded and finely chopped chillies
150g (5oz) plain (all-purpose) flour
½ tsp baking powder
¼ tsp salt
100g (3½oz) white chocolate, chopped

Preheat the oven to 180°C/160°C fan/350°F/Gas 4. Line a baking tray with baking parchment.

In a mixing bowl, combine the softened butter and condensed milk until light and fluffy. Beat in the egg and vanilla extract until well combined. Stir in the lemongrass and chillies, ensuring they are evenly distributed throughout the mixture.

In a separate bowl, sift in the flour, baking powder and salt, then whisk to combine. Gradually add this dry mixture to the wet ingredients, mixing until only just blended, without overmixing. Then gently fold in the chopped white chocolate.

Place tablespoon-sized balls of dough on the lined tray, spacing them about 5cm (2 inches) apart to allow room to spread.

Bake for 10–12 minutes, or until the edges are lightly golden. The centres should remain a little soft for a chewy texture.

Allow the cookies to cool on the tray for 5 minutes before transferring them to a wire rack to cool completely.

XÔI XOÀI

STICKY RICE WITH MANGO

TAKES 1 HOUR, PLUS SOAKING — SERVES 4

In Asian cuisine, rice in desserts is more than common; it's almost expected. This dish beautifully combines the creamy richness of coconut-infused sticky rice with the natural sweetness of ripened mango. The contrast of textures and flavours makes it even more enjoyable, showing exactly why xôi xoài is such a popular dessert across South East Asia.

200g (7oz) glutinous rice (sticky rice), soaked in water for at least 4 hours or overnight
100ml (3½fl oz) coconut milk
2 tbsp condensed milk
¼ tsp salt
1 tsp cornflour (cornstarch), dissolved in 1 tbsp water
2 ripe mangoes, peeled and sliced
2 tbsp roasted crushed pistachios

Drain the soaked glutinous rice and place it in a heatproof bowl or on a piece of muslin (cheesecloth) inside a steamer basket (or prepare in a rice cooker if you have one). Steam the rice for 30–35 minutes, until tender and sticky, checking occasionally to ensure the rice cooks evenly.

In a small pan over a medium heat, combine the coconut milk, condensed milk and salt, stirring occasionally until it begins to simmer.

Slowly add the cornflour mixture and continue to cook, stirring constantly, until the sauce thickens, then remove from the heat and set aside.

Place a generous scoop of sticky rice on each serving plate. Arrange the mango slices on top or beside the sticky rice. Drizzle the coconut sauce over the sticky rice and mango and garnish with crushed pistachios for an extra layer of flavour and texture.

Serving Suggestion
Serve this dessert fresh, allowing the warm sticky rice to soak up the creamy coconut sauce. Then sit back and enjoy it with a clean, refreshing cup of jasmine tea.

KEM CÀ PHÊ DỪA HẠT DẺ

COFFEE, COCONUT AND PISTACHIO ICE CREAM

TAKES 20 MINUTES, PLUS OVERNIGHT FREEZING — MAKES ABOUT 2 LITRES (4¼ PINTS)

All my favourite ice cream flavours in one dish! Growing up, pistachios were our family's go-to snack during TV time. We didn't have them often, so even today they still feel like a real treat. This is one of my favourite batch ice cream recipes, because making less means it always disappears too quickly!

This easy no-churn ice cream is a rich blend of coffee, condensed milk and coconut, coming together in a scoop that tastes like pure indulgence. Could it be more perfect for me? I don't think so. Try it – you can thank me later.

600ml (20fl oz/2½ cups) double (heavy) cream
300ml (10fl oz/1¼ cups) extra-thick double (heavy) cream
700ml (1½ pints/scant 3 cups) condensed milk, plus extra (optional) to serve
80g (3oz) instant coffee powder (decaf for a family-friendly version), plus extra (optional) to serve
250g (9oz) desiccated (dried shredded) coconut
50g (1¾oz) toasted coconut flakes
150g (5oz) pistachios, crushed

In a large mixing bowl, whisk both creams, the condensed milk, coffee powder and all but 20g (¾oz) of the desiccated coconut together until soft peaks form, 8–10 minutes (depending on your whisk, it might reach soft peaks sooner).

Transfer to a freezer container that has a lid, sprinkle the reserved desiccated coconut, the toasted coconut flakes and the pistachios over the top.

Freeze overnight. To serve, dust with a little coffee powder and drizzle with condensed milk for the full Vietnamese kick!

BÁNH FLAN

CRÈME CARAMEL

TAKES 1 HOUR, PLUS CHILLING — SERVES 4

Bánh flan, a lasting influence from the French colonial period, has a silky-smooth texture and balance of sweetness with a hint of bitterness from the caramel. It's a popular treat all across Vietnam: whether enjoyed as a light finish to a meal or a sweet snack, this creamy custard, topped with golden caramel, never disappoints.

100g (3½oz) caster (superfine) sugar
2 tbsp water
500ml (17fl oz/generous 2 cups) single (light) cream
4 large eggs
100ml (3½fl oz) condensed milk
1 tsp vanilla extract

Preheat the oven to 150°C/130°C fan/300°F/Gas 2.

In a small saucepan, combine the sugar and water. Heat over a medium heat, swirling the pan very gently (do not stir) until the sugar dissolves and turns deep amber. Immediately pour the caramel into four x 200ml (7fl oz) individual ramekins, tilting them to ensure an even layer of caramel in each. Set aside to cool and harden.

Rinse the pan, then use to heat the cream over a low heat until warm. Do not let it boil.

In a mixing bowl, whisk together the eggs and condensed milk until well combined. Slowly pour the warm cream into the egg mixture, whisking continuously to prevent the eggs from curdling. Then stir in the vanilla extract. Pour the custard mixture over the hardened caramel in the ramekins.

Place the ramekins in a large roasting tray, then pour hot water into the tray until it reaches halfway up the sides of the ramekins. Carefully transfer the tray to the preheated oven and bake for 45–50 minutes, until the custard is set but still slightly wobbly in the centre.

Remove the ramekins from the water bath and leave them to cool to room temperature. Then refrigerate for a minimum of 4–6 hours, or overnight for best results.

To serve, run a knife around the edges of the flan to loosen it. Invert onto a plate and carefully lift the ramekin.

Serving Suggestion

For an extra touch of indulgence, serve with a dollop of whipped cream and some fresh berries or peaches. Bánh flan pairs wonderfully with a cup of strong Vietnamese coffee, hot or iced.

BÁNH TRÁNG NƯỚNG CHUỐI SÔ-CÔ-LA

BANANA AND CHOCOLATE PANCAKES

TAKES 20 MINUTES — SERVES 4

I'm often asked if there's anything I can't make with rice paper. Honestly? Bring it on, I love the challenge! Once you've got the hang of it, rice paper reveals its magic. It's stronger than it looks, and the moment you stop worrying about how delicate it is, you'll understand why I adore cooking with it. Light, crisp, versatile and allergen free, it makes everything taste that little bit better.

This sweet treat is a firm favourite in my house and possibly the reason I wear a 'Best Mummy in the World' T-shirt with pride. It's one of those playful, feel-good recipes that invites creativity. It is a brilliantly simple dessert that's perfect for customizing – think of it like a pancake, just with a Vietnamese twist!

4 tbsp vegetable oil
4 round sheets of rice paper, 22cm (8½ inches) in diameter
4 ripe bananas, sliced
80g (3oz) chocolate chips

TO SERVE
200g (7oz) strawberries, finely diced
2 tsp unsweetened cocoa powder
Condensed milk, to drizzle (optional)
20g (¾oz) salted roasted peanuts, crushed

Heat 1 tablespoon of the oil in a frying pan (skillet).

Lightly dampen a rice paper sheet on both sides, using a clean J-cloth (food cloth). While it's still firm, place it in the hot oil.

Quickly arrange some banana slices and chocolate chips over the top – avoid piling them up. Cook for 2–3 minutes until the rice paper crisps and the chocolate melts. Fold the pancake in half and remove from the pan.

Repeat with the remaining oil, rice paper, bananas and chocolate chips.

Slice each pancake in half and top with strawberries and a dusting of cocoa powder. Drizzle with condensed milk (if using) and sprinkle with crushed peanuts to serve.

BÁNH CRUMBLE XOÀI

MANGO AND LEMONGRASS CRUMBLE

TAKES 1 HOUR — SERVES 4

This mango crumble adds a Vietnamese twist to a classic dessert, bringing together the tropical flavours of sweet mango with aromatic lemongrass, star anise and cinnamon. This warm and fragrant base is then topped with a buttery crumble and served with the classic Vietnamese coconut sauce, nước cốt dừa. All my favourite ingredients in one recipe… what's not to like?!

30g (1oz) butter
2 lemongrass stalks, crushed and cut into large pieces
5 star anise
4 large ripe mangoes, peeled and diced
125g (4½oz) brown sugar
1 tsp vanilla extract
1 tsp ground cinnamon

FOR THE CRUMBLE
100g (3½oz) plain (all-purpose) flour
50g (1¾oz) rolled oats
200g (7oz) brown sugar
75g (3oz) cold butter, cubed
½ tsp ground cinnamon

FOR THE COCONUT SAUCE
400ml (14fl oz/1¾ cups) coconut cream, at least 70% coconut
1 tbsp condensed milk
1 tsp cornflour (cornstarch), dissolved in 3 tbsp cold water
¼ tsp salt

Preheat the oven to 180°C/160°C fan/350°F/Gas 4.

In a large ovenproof pan (cast iron is ideal), melt the butter over a medium heat. Add the lemongrass and star anise and sauté for 2–3 minutes, until fragrant.

Add the diced mango and stir in the sugar, allowing it to melt into the butter and spices. Cook for 5–7 minutes until the mango softens and begins to caramelize to a golden brown. Remove the pan from the heat, discard the lemongrass and star anise and add the vanilla and cinnamon.

In a mixing bowl, combine the flour, oats and sugar. Add the cold butter cubes and, using your fingertips, rub the butter into the dry ingredients until the mixture resembles coarse crumbs. Evenly distribute the crumble topping over the mango mixture in the pan.

Bake in the oven for 40–45 minutes, until the topping is golden brown and the mango filling is bubbling.

While the crumble is baking, prepare the coconut sauce. In a small saucepan, warm the coconut cream and condensed milk, then stir in the cornflour mixture and salt. Cook over a low heat, stirring frequently, for 2–3 minutes, until slightly thickened.

Serve the crumble warm, drizzled with the coconut sauce for a perfect end to any meal, or a lovely evening treat.

BATCH COOKING CONDIMENTS

Batch cooking isn't just for professional kitchens or busy parents. It's simply smart cooking. It saves time, reduces waste and gives you more moments to enjoy your meals without the rush. Sounds good, right? That's why I recommend making these condiments before diving into the recipes in this book. Many of them call for one or more of these essentials. Having them ready at all times makes cooking effortless.

Once you're familiar with their flavours and how they enhance a dish, you'll find them useful for so many recipes beyond this book too. The best part is that every recipe in this section can be made vegetarian with just two simple swaps:

– Replace fish sauce with light soy sauce or vegan fish sauce. I prefer soy here as it has more salty umami flavour than vegan fish sauce.
– Replace oyster sauce with mushroom sauce or vegan oyster sauce.

NƯỚC CHẤM SAUCE

TAKES 15 MINUTES — MAKES 1.3 LITRES (2¾ PINTS)

The true staple of Vietnamese cuisine. Many dishes wouldn't be complete without it. It's so good that it works just as well with non-Vietnamese recipes. Once you've tasted it, this umami-rich, flavour-packed sauce will find its way onto everything you eat, from grilled (broiled) meats and fresh spring rolls to salad bowls.

900g (2lb) golden caster (superfine) sugar
600ml (20fl oz/2½ cups) warm water
300ml (10fl oz/1¼ cups) fish sauce
300ml (10fl oz/1¼ cups) lime juice
180g (6½oz) red chillies, finely chopped
 (or 50g/1¾oz bird's eye chillies)
120g (4oz) garlic, finely chopped

Add the sugar and warm water to a large bowl, stirring well until dissolved. Mix in the fish sauce and lime juice, then leave to cool.

Once completely cooled, stir in the chilli and garlic. Store in an airtight container in the fridge for up to a week.

Note

For a longer shelf life, bring the sugar, water, fish sauce and lime juice to the boil in a pan. Skim off any impurities, then leave to cool completely before adding the chilli and garlic. This version keeps for up to 3 months in the fridge.

TAMARIND SAUCE

TAKES 10 MINUTES — MAKES 1.4 LITRES (3 PINTS)

A versatile balance of natural sweet and sour flavours, perfect for seafood, stir-fries, salads and roasted vegetable dishes

900g (2lb) cane sugar
300ml (10fl oz/1¼ cups) warm water
450g (1lb) tamarind paste
500ml (17fl oz/generous 2 cups) fish sauce
180g (6½oz) red chillies, finely chopped
 (or 50g/1¾oz bird's eye chillies)
120g (4oz) garlic, finely chopped

Add the sugar and warm water to a large bowl, stirring well until dissolved. Mix in the tamarind paste and fish sauce, then leave to cool.

Once completely cooled, stir in the chilli and garlic. Store in an airtight container in the fridge for up to a week.

Note

For a longer shelf life, bring the sugar, water, tamarind paste and fish sauce to the boil in a pan. Skim off any impurities, then leave to cool completely before adding the chilli and garlic. This version keeps for up to 3 months in the fridge.

ROASTED GARLIC OIL

TAKES 30 MINUTES, PLUS INFUSING — MAKES 300ML (10FL OZ/1¼ CUPS)

This recipe makes a full jar of roasted garlic oil, but often you will only use a small amount. You could make just enough for the recipe, but it's impractical, and making a batch takes no more time. In fact, I'd recommend doubling or even tripling it. It stores well and adds magic to nearly any dish. After all, who doesn't love garlic?

3 garlic bulbs
3 red chillies
200ml (7fl oz) olive oil

Preheat the oven to 200°C/180°C fan (400°F) Gas 6. Slice the tops off the garlic bulbs and, leaving the chillies whole, roast together on a baking tray for 25–30 minutes.

Once cooled, peel the garlic and place it along with the chillies into a 300ml (10fl oz/1¼ cups) jar, then fill with the olive oil. Leave to infuse for 3–4 days for best results, although using it immediately will still be delicious. It can be stored in a cool, dark place for up to 6 months.

SWEET SOY SAUCE

TAKES 15 MINUTES — MAKES 1.3 LITRES (2¾ PINTS)

A rich, deeply flavoured, all-purpose vegan sauce that adds umami to everything from vegetables and tofu to meat. Perfect for drizzling, dipping or stir-frying, it brings a savoury-sweet balance to any dish.

500ml (17fl oz/generous 2 cups) light soy sauce
500ml (17fl oz/generous 2 cups) lime juice
1kg (2lb 4oz) golden caster (superfine) sugar
180g (6½oz) red chillies, finely chopped (or 50g/1¾oz bird's eye chillies)
120g (4oz) garlic, finely chopped

Add the soy sauce, lime juice and sugar to a large bowl, stirring well until dissolved.

Stir in the chilli and garlic. Store in an airtight container in the fridge for up to a week.

Note
For a longer shelf life, bring the soy sauce, lime juice and sugar to the boil in a pan. Skim off any impurities, then leave to cool completely before adding the chilli and garlic. This version keeps for up to 3 months in the fridge.

GINGER AND CHIVE OIL

TAKES 20 MINUTES — MAKES 500ML (17FL OZ/ GENEROUS 2 CUPS)

This fragrant finishing oil enhances simple dishes with its aromatic richness. Drizzle over vegetables, fish, meat, noodles or rice for an instant flavour boost, but be sure to scoop up some of the chives at the bottom of the jar too!

400ml (14fl oz/1¾ cups) vegetable oil
200g (7oz) ginger, peeled and finely diced (see note)
100g (3½oz) chives, chopped
1 tsp salt
2 tbsp light soy sauce

Heat the oil in a pan over a medium-high heat until it reaches 150°C (302°F). To check if the oil is ready, dip a wooden chopstick into it. If bubbles form around the chopstick, it's ready.

Remove from the heat, then stir in the ginger, chives, salt and soy sauce.

Leave the mixture to cool before transferring to an airtight container. Store in the fridge for up to 3 months.

Note
To dice the ginger, peel and slice using a mandolin, then cut the slices into thin strips lengthways before cutting across into dice.

CHILLI AND LEMONGRASS OIL

TAKES 30 MINUTES — MAKES 1 LITRE (34FL OZ/ GENEROUS 4 CUPS)

The sauce that works with everything! Fragrant, with the perfect amount of heat. Great for stir-fries, noodles, grilled (broiled) meats, baked potatoes or even a pasta bake. My personal favourite way to serve it is with a cheese board. I always have a big jar ready.

2 tbsp vegetable oil
100g (3½oz) lemongrass, finely chopped
50g (1¾oz) shallots, finely chopped
50g (1¾oz) garlic, finely chopped
100g (3½oz) chilli flakes
50g (1¾oz) chilli powder
200g (7oz) cane sugar
200ml (7fl oz) light soy sauce
100ml (3½fl oz) fish sauce
500ml (17fl oz/generous 2 cups) sesame oil

Heat the vegetable oil in a pan over a medium-high heat. Add the lemongrass and shallots and sauté for 3–4 minutes, until browned.

Stir in the garlic and cook for 1 minute. Add the chilli flakes, chilli powder, sugar, soy sauce and fish sauce, mixing well. Pour in the sesame oil and cook gently over a medium heat for 5 minutes, allowing the flavours to meld together perfectly.

Remove from heat and leave to cool. Once cooled completely, pour into an airtight container and store in the fridge for up to 3 months.

Batch Cooking Condiments

CRISPY FRIED SHALLOTS

TAKES 45 MINUTES — MAKES 500G (1LB 2OZ)

Golden, fragrant and irresistibly crunchy, crispy fried shallots add the perfect finishing touch to soups, noodles, rice dishes and salads.

1 litre (34fl oz/generous 4 cups) vegetable oil
1kg (2lb 4oz) shallots, very finely chopped

Heat the oil in a large, deep frying pan (skillet) over a medium heat, until it reaches 150–160°C (302–320°F). To check if it's ready, place a wooden chopstick into the oil: if bubbles form around it, the oil is at the right temperature.

Fry the shallots in batches of around 100g (3½oz), stirring occasionally, until golden brown.

Remove with a skimmer and drain on paper towels, repeating the process until all the shallots have been cooked. Leave them on the paper towels overnight to air-dry, helping to preserve their crispness.

Once completely dry, transfer to an airtight container and store in a cool, dry place for up to a month.

DAIKON AND CARROT PICKLE

TAKES 15 MINUTES — MAKES: 500G (1LB 2OZ)

A classic Vietnamese pickle that brings a crisp, tangy crunch to bánh mì, rice dishes and noodle bowls. Simple yet essential for a Vietnamese meal, it plays a key role in balancing the five fundamental flavours (see page 12). Having a jar of this in the fridge makes it easy to liven up your meal in seconds.

400ml (14fl oz/1¾ cups) lime juice (or rice wine vinegar)
300g (10½oz) caster (superfine) sugar
200g (7oz) carrots, julienned
200g (7oz) daikon, julienned

Heat the lime juice and sugar in a pan over a medium heat, stirring until the sugar has completely dissolved. Remove from the heat and leave to cool completely.

Place the carrots and daikon in a sterilized jar and pour the cooled sweet lime mixture over the vegetables, ensuring they are fully submerged.

Seal the jar and refrigerate for at least a day, or up to 3 days for maximum flavour.

Store in the fridge for up to a month.

ALL-PURPOSE MARINADE

TAKES 5 MINUTES — MAKES 1.6 LITRES (3½ PINTS)

The ultimate marinade for infusing depth, richness and balanced flavour into a dish. A perfect blend of savoury, sweet and aromatic elements, it works beautifully with beef, chicken, pork or even tofu. Whether grilling (broiling), roasting or pan-searing, this marinade guarantees tender, flavour-packed results every time. The perfect answer to fuss-free barbecues all summer long!

500g (1lb 2oz) oyster sauce
500ml (17fl oz/generous 2 cups) light soy sauce
200g (7oz) coarsely ground black pepper
300ml (10fl oz/1¼ cups) sesame oil
100g (3½oz) garlic powder
100g (3½oz) chilli powder

In a large bowl, mix all the ingredients together until smooth. Pour into an airtight container and store in the fridge for up to 3 weeks.

INDEX

A

apples
    roast pork & nước chấm apple salsa 114–15
    sweet & sour beef salad 142–3
apricot, & shaking chicken salad 138
aubergine, curry leaf, & shiitake mushroom 156–7
autumn rolls, prawn & wild mushroom 32–3
avocado
    avocado toast 30–1
    pomelo & prawn pea shoot salad 140–1

B

bacon & prawn quiche 60–1
bamboo shoots, & braised pork & quail's eggs 100–1
bamboo steamer, use of 18
banana & chocolate pancakes 170–1
bean sprouts
    'beef phở' flatbread wrap 34–5
    the joy pancake 56–7
beef
    beef fillet phở soup 66–7
    'beef phở' flatbread wrap 34–5
    beef skewers & peanut sauce 45
    chilli marmalade brisket bánh mì 42–3
    'full Vietnamese' breakfast 54–5
    osso buco lemongrass stew 96–7
    red-hot short ribs 112–13
    spaghetti bolognese 80–1
    sweet & sour beef salad 142–3
bolognese, spaghetti 80–1
braising, technique 16, 18
breakfast, 'full Vietnamese' 54–5
brisket, & chilli marmalade bánh mì 42–3
burger, pork & prawn chả giò 48–9
butternut squash & coconut soup 78–9

C

cabbage
    charred cabbage with 'sốt tưởng ngọt' peanut sauce 149
    crispy butter chicken salad 146–7
    roast duck noodle soup 70–1
calamari *see* squid
carbonara, udon 86–7
carrot & daikon pickle, how to make 180
carrots
    charcuterie summer rolls 36–7
    crispy butter chicken salad 146–7
    honey-roasted carrots in bo´ sauce 148
    osso buco lemongrass stew 96–7
    roast duck noodle soup 70–1
    spaghetti bolognese 80–1
cauliflower, baked chimichurri 158
cavolo nero & roasted garlic stir fry 150–1
cheese
    bacon & prawn quiche 60–1
    salted peanut & coffee cheesecake 162–3
    udon carbonara 86–7
chestnuts
    fried chicken spring rolls 39
    pork & prawn chả giò burger 48–9
chicken
    chicken glass noodle soup 72–3
    chilli marmalade brisket bánh mì 42–3
    crispy butter chicken salad 146–7
    fried chicken spring rolls 39
    'full Vietnamese' breakfast 54–5
    garlic fish sauce wings 104–5
    ginger caramelized chicken 106–7
    lemongrass & coconut chicken curry 102–3
    lemongrass chicken noodle bowl 84–5
    prawn & chive diamond dumplings 58–9
    rotisserie spatchcock chicken 92
    shaking chicken & apricot salad 138

chicory
    crab, kohlrabi & dill mustard salad 139
    pork & seafood noodle soup 68–9
chilli & lemongrass oil, how to make 179
chilli chocolate cookies 164
chillies, description 24
chimichurri, baked, cauliflower 158
chives, description 24
chocolate
    banana & chocolate pancakes 170–1
    chilli chocolate cookies 164
chorizo
    avocado toast 30–1
    garlic & lạp xưởng egg noodles 83
clay pot
    clay pot hake 120–1
    use of 20
clementines
    clementine, pear & peach lemongrass duck 110–11
    kiwi & clementine tuna ceviche 124–5
coconut
    description 22
    butternut squash & coconut soup 78–9
    clay pot hake 120–1
    coffee, coconut & pistachio ice cream 166–7
    creamy sweet potato & wild mushrooms 159
    ginger caramelized chicken 106–7
    the joy pancake 56–7
    lemongrass & coconut chicken curry 102–3
    mango & lemongrass crumble 172–3
    mussels in coconut cream 126–7
    seafood & coconut udon 76–7
    spiced lamb shank stew 93
    sticky rice with mango 165

cod
    cod & chive potato fish cakes 122–3
    pan-fried cod in tomato salsa 132–3
coffee
    coffee, coconut & pistachio ice cream 166–7
    salted peanut & coffee cheesecake 162–3
cookies, chilli chocolate 164
cornflour (cornstarch), description 22
courgettes
    clementine, pear & peach lemongrass duck 110–11
    courgette & prawn soup 89
crab
    crab, kohlrabi & dill mustard salad 139
    fried chicken spring rolls 39
    seafood rice crackers 52–3
cream
    bacon & prawn quiche 60–1
    coffee, coconut & pistachio ice cream 166–7
    salted peanut & coffee cheesecake 162–3
crème caramel 168–9
crispy fried shallots
    description 22
    how to make 180
crumble, mango & lemongrass 172–3
cucumber
    charcuterie summer rolls 36–7
    crispy butter chicken salad 146–7
    'full Vietnamese' breakfast 54–5
    grilled pork rice 108–9
    lemongrass chicken noodle bowl 84–5
    sweet & sour beef salad 142–3

D

daikon & carrot pickle, how to make 180
dover sole, baked, fish sauce butter 130–1
duck
    clementine, pear & peach lemongrass duck 110–11
    confit duck watermelon salad 136–7
    roast duck noodle soup 70–1
    spiced roast duck 117
dumplings, prawn & chive diamond 58–9

E

eggplant, shiitake mushroom & curry leaf 156–7
eggs
    avocado toast 30–1
    bacon & prawn quiche 60–1
    braised pork, quail's eggs & bamboo shoots 100–1
    crème caramel 168–9
    fried chicken spring rolls 39
    'full Vietnamese' breakfast 54–5
    garlic & lạp xưởng egg noodles 83
    grilled pork rice 108–9
    honey-roasted carrots in bo' sauce 148
    the joy pancake 56–7
    king oyster & tomato noodle soup 75
    pork & prawn chả giò burger 48–9
    pork & seafood noodle soup 68–9
    prawn & chive diamond dumplings 58–9
    udon carbonara 86–7

F

fennel: crab, kohlrabi & dill mustard salad 139
fire cooking, technique 19
fish, fried, with crispy tamarind & red onion 144–5
fish cakes, cod & chive potato 122–3
fish sauce, description 23
flatbread wrap, 'beef phở' 34–5

G

garlic
    description 24
    garlic & lạp xưởng egg noodles 83
    garlic fish sauce wings 104–5
    roasted garlic oil, how to make 178
    roasted garlic stir fry & cavolo nero 150–1
ginger
    description 24
    ginger & chive oil, how to make 179
    ginger caramelized chicken 106–7
    ginger silken tofu 62–3

H

hake, clay pot 120–1
herb butter, sea bream with lemongrass & 128–9
honey
    description 23
    honey & chilli pork tacos 50–1
    honey-roasted carrots in bo' sauce 148

K

kale: cavolo nero & roasted garlic stir fry 150–1
kiwi & clementine tuna ceviche 124–5
kohlrabi, & crab dill mustard salad 139

L

lamb shank stew, spiced 93
lemongrass
    description 24
    lemongrass & coconut chicken curry 102–3
    lemongrass chicken noodle bowl 84–5
    osso buco lemongrass stew 96–7
    sea bream with lemongrass & herb butter 128–9
lemons
    baked dover sole, fish sauce butter 130–1
    sea bream with lemongrass & herb butter 128–9

lettuce
    confit duck watermelon salad 136–7
    grilled pork rice 108–9
    the joy pancake 56–7
    lemongrass chicken noodle bowl 84–5
    shaking chicken & apricot salad 138
lime
    description 23
    avocado toast 30–1
    'beef phở' flatbread wrap 34–5
    charred cabbage with 'sốt tương ngọt'
    peanut sauce 119
    chicken glass noodle soup 72–3
    crispy tamarind & red onion fried fish 144–5
    kiwi & clementine tuna ceviche 124–5
    nước chấm sauce 175
    sweet soy sauce, how to make 178
lime leaves, description 24

M

mangetout: sweet & sour beef salad 142–3
mango
    the joy pancake 56–7
    mango & lemongrass crumble 172–3
    pomelo & prawn pea shoot salad 140–1
    sticky rice with mango 165
    sweet & sour beef salad 142–3
marinade, all-purpose, how to make 181
marmalade, chilli, & brisket bánh mì 42–3
mushrooms
    bacon & prawn quiche 60–1
    chilli marmalade brisket bánh mì 42–3
    creamy sweet potato & wild mushrooms 159
    fried chicken spring rolls 39
    king oyster & tomato noodle soup 75
    osso buco lemongrass stew 96–7
    oyster mushrooms sautéed in turmeric butter 154–5
    pan-fried cod in tomato salsa 132–3
    pork & prawn chả giò burger 48–9

    prawn & wild mushroom autumn rolls 32–3
    shiitake mushroom & curry leaf aubergine 156–7
    tofu huế-style noodle soup 74
mussels in coconut cream 126–7

N

noodles
    bacon & prawn quiche 60–1
    chicken glass noodle soup 72–3
    fried chicken spring rolls 39
    garlic & lạp xưởng egg noodles 83
    king oyster & tomato noodle soup 75
    lemongrass chicken noodle bowl 84–5
    pork & prawn chả giò burger 48–9
    pork & seafood noodle soup 68–9
    roast duck noodle soup 70–1
    seafood & coconut udon 76–7
    smoked tofu garlic-tossed sweet potato vermicelli 82
    spaghetti bolognese 80–1
    tofu huế-style noodle soup 74
    udon carbonara 86–7
nước chấm sauce
    description 23
    how to make 175
    roast pork & nước chấm apple salsa 114–15

O

osso buco lemongrass stew 96–7
oyster sauce
    description 23
    all-purpose marinade, how to make 181

P

pancakes
    banana & chocolate pancakes 170–1
    the joy pancake 56–7
pancetta: udon carbonara 86–7
paprika, description 23
parsnips: osso buco lemongrass stew 96–7

peach, pear & clementine lemongrass duck 110–11
peanuts
   description 24
   beef skewers & peanut sauce 45
   charred cabbage with 'sốt tưởng ngọt' peanut sauce 149
   salted peanut & coffee cheesecake 162–3
pear, clementine & peach lemongrass duck 110–11
pea shoots
   the joy pancake 56–7
   pomelo & prawn pea shoot salad 140–1
peppers
   charcuterie summer rolls 36–7
   pan-fried cod in tomato salsa 132–3
perilla: pomelo & prawn pea shoot salad 140–1
pineapple
   the joy pancake 56–7
   silken tofu, tomato & pineapple soup 88
pistachios
   coffee, coconut & pistachio ice cream 166–7
   sticky rice with mango 165
pomelo & prawn pea shoot salad 140–1
pork
   braised pork, quail's eggs & bamboo shoots 100–1
   chilli marmalade brisket bánh mì 42–3
   crackling tips 116
   'full Vietnamese' breakfast 54–5
   grilled pork rice 108–9
   grilled pork skewers 44
   honey & chilli pork tacos 50–1
   pork & prawn chả giò burger 48–9
   pork & seafood noodle soup 68–9
   roast pork & nước chấm apple salsa 114–15
   sticky pork ribs 98–9
potatoes
   cod & chive potato fish cakes 122–3
   lemongrass & coconut chicken curry 102–3

prawns
   bacon & prawn quiche 60–1
   courgette & prawn soup 89
   the joy pancake 56–7
   pomelo & prawn pea shoot salad 140–1
   pork & prawn chả giò burger 48–9
   pork & seafood noodle soup 68–9
   prawn & chive diamond dumplings 58–9
   prawn & wild mushroom autumn rolls 32–3
   prawn-stuffed baked heirloom tomatoes 152–3
   seafood rice crackers 52–3

Q
quiche, bacon & prawn 60–1

R
radishes: honey & chilli pork tacos 50–1
red onions, & crispy tamarind fried fish 144–5
rice
   description 23
   grilled pork rice 108–9
   sticky rice with mango 165
rice cooker, use of
rice crackers, seafood 52–3
rice noodles, description 23
rice paper, how to use 38
rice wine vinegar, description 23
rocket: the joy pancake 56–7

S
sauces, batch-cooking 26
   see also under individual sauces
sausages
   avocado toast 30–1
   garlic & lạp xưởng egg noodles 83
scallions, description 24
seabass: crispy tamarind & red onion fried fish 144–5
sea bream with lemongrass & herb butter 128–9

seafood & coconut udon 76–7
sesame oil, description 23
shallots, description 24
shrimp paste, description 23
shrimps see prawns
soup
    beef fillet phở soup 66–7
    butternut squash & coconut soup 78–9
    chicken glass noodle soup 72–3
    courgette & prawn soup 89
    king oyster & tomato noodle soup 75
    pork & seafood noodle soup 68–9
    roast duck noodle soup 70–1
    seafood & coconut udon 76–7
    silken tofu, tomato & pineapple soup 88
    tofu huê´-style noodle soup 74
soy sauce
    description 23
    sweet, how to make 178
spring onions, description 24
spring rolls, fried chicken 39
squid
    pork & seafood noodle soup 68–9
    seafood & coconut udon 76–7
star fruit: the joy pancake 56–7
steamer (bamboo or metal), use of 20
steaming, technique 18
stir-frying, technique 16
strawberries, banana & chocolate pancakes 170–1
sugar
    golden cane, description 23
    rock, description 23
summer rolls, charcuterie 36–7
sweet potatoes
    creamy sweet potato & wild mushrooms 159
    smoked tofu garlic-tossed sweet potato vermicelli 82

T
tacos, honey & chilli pork 50–1
tamarind, description 23
tamarind sauce
    how to make 175
    crispy tamarind & red onion fried fish 144–5
tofu
    avocado toast 30–1
    charcuterie summer rolls 36–7
    ginger silken tofu 62–3
    the joy pancake 56–7
    king oyster & tomato noodle soup 75
    silken tofu, tomato & pineapple soup 88
    smoked tofu garlic-tossed sweet potato vermicelli 82
    tofu huê´-style noodle soup 74
tomatoes
    avocado toast 30–1
    'full Vietnamese' breakfast 54–5
    grilled pork rice 108–9
    king oyster & tomato noodle soup 75
    pan-fried cod in tomato salsa 132–3
    prawn-stuffed baked heirloom tomatoes 152–3
    red-hot short ribs 112–13
    shaking chicken & apricot salad 138
    silken tofu, tomato & pineapple soup 88
    spaghetti bolognese 80–1
    sweet & sour beef salad 142–3
tuna ceviche, & kiwi & clementine 124–5

U
umami paste, description 23

W
watermelon salad, & confit duck 136–7
wonton wrappers: prawn & chive diamond dumplings 58–9

Z
zucchini see courgettes

Index

ABOUT THE AUTHOR

Born in a small village in the south of Vietnam, Thuy's childhood was surrounded by food and her love of cooking started early. At the age of just seven, Thuy was proudly trusted with the heavy responsibility of cooking the family rice. As a grandchild of farmers, she grew up amid a wonderful variety of fruits hanging from trees, morning markets with freshly picked vegetables, and the amazing smells of traditional street food. It's these memories that are the foundation of her food philosophy.

Thuy's father was a naval commander and one of the Southern Vietnamese 'boat people' who, after the war, risked everything by putting out to sea in the hope of reaching international waters. With no possibility of an education for his children in a post-war Vietnam, he felt this was the only hope for their future. He was one of the lucky ones, rescued by an English ship and granted asylum, and eventually managed to bring his family over, five long years later, when Thuy was seven years old.

After fulfilling her parents' dream of earning a degree, Thuy spent the best part of a decade building a career in marketing, climbing the corporate ladder and eventually running her own international agency. She was later awarded an honorary doctorate in Business Administration by her university, in recognition of her contributions to business and entrepreneurship. However, cooking was always her passion, and she finally found the courage to take the plunge and chase her own dream. Ten years later, having founded and run the multi-award-winning The Little Viet Kitchen, Thuy is renowned as the UK's most prominent authority on Vietnamese cuisine.

She now shares her culinary passion nationwide as a chef consultant, representing brands such as Rangemaster, Kamado Joe, Gozney and TOG knives, while proudly serving as a judge for esteemed awards such as the Guild of Food Writers Awards, the BaxterStorey People Awards, and The Golden Chopsticks, Asian Cuisine Awards. With her cookbooks, Thuy continues to delight food enthusiasts across the globe with the broad appeal of her delicious yet attainable recipes.

At The Little Viet Kitchen, Thuy perfected a dining experience that seamlessly merged restaurant precision with the comfort of home cooking, creating a unique approach to Vietnamese cuisine in the West. Drawing on her authentic understanding of Vietnamese culture and a local's insight into London's evolving food scene, she has left a lasting mark on the culinary landscape.

Since moving on from her restaurant, Thuy has grown beyond the confines of her kitchen, captivating audiences at major food festivals, on television shows such as *MasterChef*, *Saturday Kitchen*, *Ainsley Harriot's Fantastic Flavours*, and Nadiya Hussain's *Cook Once Eat Twice*, and through residencies at prestigious five-star hotels and resorts.

ACKNOWLEDGEMENTS

Cooking has long been my way of expressing myself. Food is my love language. The whole process mirrors who I am: the strategic planning, the meticulous care in my *mise en place*, the joy I find in selecting the perfect produce, the care I take over presentation, the satisfaction that comes from creating something, and the pleasure in making people happy (and full). Choosing to cook and showcase Vietnamese cuisine is my way of honouring my heritage, embracing my past, living my present, and shaping the future of the food I love.

If you know me well, you'll know I can talk for hours… And when it comes to food? Days. English is my second language, so becoming an author and finding therapy in writing was never something I imagined possible. But here I am, thanks to my high school English teacher, Kate Chapman. Your class was the hardest but also the most enjoyable. You always had the time and patience for that painfully shy, insecure teenage Thuy. You influenced me more than you'll ever know. Thank you, Ms Chapman. As I write this, my third book, you came to mind, and I hope you know how important your role is to the lives of your students after they leave your classroom.

Now on to the acknowledgements. The thank yous! The part where I inevitably worry about forgetting someone I shouldn't. For me, every book is a new experience, a time-stamped chapter in both my life and my food journey.

To my little family, **Dave** and **Jacob Xôi**. Not only are you my daily inspiration to be better, but our life together also inspires the recipes in these pages. The hours I've poured into this book? You've matched them, if not more, supporting me so I could test, write, eat and repeat (endlessly). Dave, thank you for the extra daddy daycare sessions, for understanding my writer's block stares and for disappearing on cue, as fast as a toddler allows, so I could capture a passing thought. Honestly, you boys are pros now. Time will keep flying by, too quickly for my liking, but you will always be my number one priority. Let's keep making memories, and let's make them delicious.

Mum and Dad, the words "thank you" could never be enough, but here they are. Your love for me and my siblings has always been clear, not through cards or cuddly hugs, but through the selfless sacrifices you've made, time and time again. I hope we've made you proud. Now, as a parent myself, I finally understand what real love means and it only makes me love you both more. At every major chapter of my life, every big event, you've been there right at the forefront, supporting me. When I launched the restaurant, Dad, you stepped in as kitchen porter, and Mum, you jumped on every section that needed you. Mum, your spring rolls are still the best I've ever tasted, perfectly rolled, no shortcuts. Your quiet mastery in the kitchen makes Vietnamese cooking look effortless, but we both know it takes a lifetime to truly understand the balance and beauty of our cuisine. Your honest, humble approach to food, and the respect you show every ingredient is what makes you the true master. I hope to carry your teachings forward and make you proud. Watching how much Jacob Xôi adores his ông bà ngoại melts my heart. I promise to keep raising him on the fluffiest rice, properly balanced fish sauce, and lots of fresh herbs, just as it should be.

To the many chefs I've had the pleasure of working with, you know who you are. This one's for you! There has not been a single week over the past few years where I've not either been next to, or joining forces with you, to cook up a storm in kitchens up and down the country. From small kitchens with no space and little equipment, to large fancy 'chef's dream kitchen' spaces, we still prepare food the proper way, respectfully and with much love and care. You continue to amaze me, and your passion makes work a joy. You're definitely made of different stuff, and I love it. Not everyone will fully appreciate your hard work and dedication, but that's okay. As long as it still fills your heart with joy to bring smiles to those eating your food, then our mission is accomplished.

To my industry friends, we have the most important thing in common, our love of food, so that already makes you a special human in my life!

Frank Coughlan, the cool big brother I never had. Your floral shirts put my wardrobe to shame, and your chicken-skewering skills remain undefeated, but above all, you have a heart of gold. Thank you, chef. This chapter of my career would have looked very different without your support.

Andy Aston, it was fate that we met, and now you're stuck with me, hahaha! You've shown me that kindness can live alongside chaos in this manic industry. Your selfless work for charities and chefs across the country sets a standard for all of us, especially the next generation. I'm so grateful to call you a friend, Aston. Thank you, chef.

Ben Forte, what can I say? Some of the best friendships are forged around the fire pit, and ours is no exception. It was sealed when you grilled 700kg of chicken thighs on that spectacular row of Kamado Joes. That says it all, you're a true grill hero, and you didn't quit at 699kg! Thank you for always backing me through every wild idea (let's call it passion) and for always following through. Your work ethic is your super power, but your big heart is the real secret. Jacob absolutely adores Uncle Hairy Ben, which makes you family in our book!

Elly James, Thank you for being the calm in every storm and the voice of reason whenever I felt like losing my head. Your support has never wavered: steadfast when I've needed it most, and just as strong when I didn't realise I needed it at all. I'm so lucky to have had you in my corner for this. You've been amazing.

Stacey Cleworth, our second baby! This book wouldn't exist without you. From the day we met, you've kept your word and placed your faith in me and in Vietnamese cuisine. The energy you bring always leaves me buzzing, and it stayed with me even when you were on the other side of the world. I hope you're as proud of 'One Pan Vietnam' as I am. Even from afar, you've always been part of the team. Thank you, you're an amazing human.

Laura, **Joss**, **Tabs** and **El**, another one bites the dust! Baby number two together, and it's perfect. Laura, you capture magic with such ease (we know it's not). Joss, your salad tosses and off-the-plate drizzles make pages you want to lick. Tabs, your dancing and joy fills every room and frame. El, you run the show with grace and just the right amount of mischief. What we made, with sunshine, laughter, and apron-off moments, was pure magic.

Kajal, **Sally**, **Claire**, **Sofie** and **Alicia**, thank you for making my dream pages come alive! Your care and craft brought it all together so beautifully. It's been a pleasure to share the love for Vietnamese cuisine with you, and your support has helped me record this new chapter in my food journey! Cheers to that, ladies!

All my love,
Thuy xxx

Quadrille, Penguin Random House UK, One Embassy Gardens, 8 Viaduct Gardens, London SW11 7BW

Quadrille Publishing Limited is part of the Penguin Random House group of companies whose addresses can be found at global.penguinrandomhouse.com

Text ©Thuy Diem Pham 2026
Photography ©Laura Edwards 2026
Illustrations © Claire Rochford 2026
Design and Layout © Quadrille 2026

Thuy Diem Pham has asserted her right to be identified as the author(s) of this Work in accordance with the Copyright, Designs and Patents Act 1988

Penguin Random House values and supports copyright. Copyright fuels creativity, encourages diverse voices, promotes freedom of expression and supports a vibrant culture. Thank you for purchasing an authorized edition of this book and for respecting intellectual property laws by not reproducing, scanning or distributing any part of it by any means without permission. You are supporting authors and enabling Penguin Random House to continue to publish books for everyone. No part of this book may be used or reproduced in any manner for the purpose of training artificial intelligence technologies or systems. In accordance with Article 4(3) of the DSM Directive 2019/790, Penguin Random House expressly reserves this work from the text and data mining exception.

Published by Quadrille in 2026

www.penguin.co.uk

A CIP catalogue record for this book is available from the British Library

ISBN 978 1 83783 329 0
10 9 8 7 6 5 4 3 2 1

Managing Director, Publishing Sarah Lavelle
Publishing Director Kajal Mistry
Senior Commissioning Editor Stacey Cleworth
Editor Sofie Shearman
Copy Editor Sally Somers
Proofreader Stephanie Evans
Design Manager Katherine Case
Designers Claire Rochford and Alicia House
Photographer Laura Edwards
Props Stylist Tabitha Hawkins
Food Stylist Joss Herd
Food Stylist Assistant El Kemp
Head of Production Stephen Lang
Production Manager Sabeena Atchia

Colour reproduction by p2d

Printed in China by C&C Offset Printing Co., Ltd.

The authorised representative in the EEA is Penguin Random House Ireland, Morrison Chambers, 32 Nassau Street, Dublin D02 YH68.

Penguin Random House is committed to a sustainable future for our business, our readers and our planet. This book is made from Forest Stewardship Council® certified paper.